OUTRAGED

OUTRAGED

Ashley 'Dotty' Charles

BLOOMSBURY PUBLISHING

NEW YORK · LONDON · OXFORD · NEW DELHI · SYDNEY

BLOOMSBURY PUBLISHING
Bloomsbury Publishing Inc.
1385 Broadway, New York, NY 10018, USA

BLOOMSBURY, BLOOMSBURY PUBLISHING, and the Diana
logo are trademarks of Bloomsbury Publishing Plc

First published in 2020 in Great Britain
First published in the United States 2020

ISBN: HB: 978-1-63557-500-2; eBook: 978-1-63557-501-9

Library of Congress Cataloging-in-Publication Data is available.

2 4 6 8 10 9 7 5 3 1

Typeset by Newgen KnowledgeWorks Pvt. Ltd., Chennai, India
Printed and bound in the U.S.A. by Berryville Graphics Inc., Berryville, Virginia

To find out more about our authors and books visit
www.bloomsbury.com and sign up for our newsletters.

Bloomsbury books may be purchased for business or promotional use.
For information on bulk purchases please contact Macmillan Corporate and
Premium Sales Department at specialmarkets@macmillan.com.

CONTENTS

PROLOGUE

I never should have checked my phone on holiday. But there I was, in sun-drenched Thailand, scrolling through Twitter, incapable of detaching myself from the Internet. As a radio presenter and therefore an ego-maniac by default, the thought of disconnecting from my 'platforms' was an unspeakable horror that I could only endure for so long, so I settled in like the social media crackhead I am, ready to get my fix.

We were ten days into our two-week trip; we being my assorted biscuit tin of a family: me, my fiancée Lina and our six-month-old son Camden, who had impressively made it through his first long-haul flight with minimal screaming and therefore only marginal embarrassment to his mums. We were the picture of gaycation bliss.

The fun tourist leg of our trip had started in Phuket and we were now at the business end of our stay – an obligatory pit stop at Lina's family home in Nong Khai. She'd warned me that her army of aunts would assemble the moment we arrived, expecting us (I assumed) to present our baby to the congregation *Lion King* style. And, right on cue, what I can only guess was the entire population of the village appeared in her mother's driveway, eager for a first glimpse at our sperm-donor baby.

'You guys said he would be black,' said a disappointed family member, who hadn't quite got to grips with biracial genetics, presuming perhaps that 'black' only comes in one shade.

Overwhelmed and already out of words (my grasp of the Thai language starts and ends with 'sawadee ka'), I made my excuses and escaped inside, leaving Lina to answer the intrusive questions without me, and our infant son to fend for himself under a swarm of cheek-pinchers and well-wishers.

I closed the bedroom door, which only slightly muffled the commotion outside and, basking in the air con, wondered how I could kill an hour while a never-ending conveyor belt of aunties played pass the parcel with my firstborn. There was no harm in checking how my social media stats were doing, I thought, surely my tree-house view from Kamala Beach had notched up a few hundred likes on Instagram by now. You see, when it comes to social networking I'm a lurker more than a poster. My snoop-to-share ratio is weighted so heavily on the former you could actually be fooled into thinking I have better things to do than refresh my feed every thirty minutes. I absolutely don't. So on those sporadic occasions when I actually post something I obsess over its performance, neurotically overthinking how well it will be received and intermittently monitoring its feedback. Because in a world where adulation is king, GOD FORBID I ever end up sharing a picture that gets less than 500 likes.

But I never should have checked my phone on holiday.

H&M is CANCELLED!

H&M have you lost your damned minds?!?!?!

Please retweet to spread the word on this racist company #BoycottHandM #HandMisRacist

I'd walked into the middle of an online feeding frenzy, one of those occasional social media moments where everyone is shouting about the same thing. But this wasn't political commentary or *Game of Thrones* spoilers, it was an uprising of some sort. And by the looks of things, the wall-to-wall fury was of the high-street clothes store variety. A niche subgenre of outrage if ever I'd seen one. I swiped curiously through my Twitter feed, eager to catch up with the conversation that everyone seemed to be having. *This must be bad*, I salivated, so desensitised to communal outrage that it now contributed to my daily intake of online entertainment.

I scrolled past dozens of angry tweets and finally landed on the one that seemed to have started it all. The original post by @nerdabouttown included a picture pulled from the H&M website. 'COOLEST MONKEY IN THE JUNGLE' read the iron-on text printed on the rather cheap-looking H&M hoody. It was modelled by a handsome young black boy who looked no more than six years old.

'I'm fucking disgusted. Like… what was the thought process behind this [H&M]???' read one of @nerdabouttown's follow-up tweets.

And she wasn't the only one up in arms.

'Woke up this morning shocked and embarrassed by this photo. I'm deeply offended and will not be working with H&M any more,' posted musician and H&M brand partner The Weeknd in a searing tweet that was also doing the rounds.

'Wait, is that it?' I asked myself out loud. *This* is the H&M hoody that everyone's furious about? *This* is the 'deeply offensive' picture that prompted The Weeknd to

cancel his brand endorsement? THIS?!! This £7.99 piece of
fabric that probably won't have any words on it at all after
two cycles in the washing machine? There's got to be more
to it, I thought as I continued to trawl through tweets.

There wasn't.

I paused for thought. Maybe I was being too casual about
the whole thing. Ten days in a tropical climate will work
wonders for your patience, so maybe the Singha beers and
water sports had just heightened my outrage threshold.
I probably wasn't looking at the hoody properly. So
I zoomed in on it. I zoomed back out. I looked at it full-
screen. I looked at it sideways.

*It is kinda offensive, I guess. Why has the black kid gotta be the
monkey?* I thought, forcing my tribalism to kick in. That
social instinct that urges you to speak up for your own in
times of moral unrest. An unspoken allegiance between
skinfolk that has, for generations, been a means of sur-
vival. The sort of blind loyalty that has had me defending
Tyler Perry's dog-shit movies for years simply because he's
one of us.

I felt like I was supposed to be angry too. *But maybe the
black kid is wearing the monkey hoody because nobody at H&M
associated it with race,* said an uninvited voice in my head.
*Maybe it says more about our expectations of racism than it does
about any actual intentions of racism,* the voice continued,
contradicting everything I thought I was meant to be
feeling.

'Have you seen this H&M hoody?' I texted my mum,
completely forgetting that I was supposed to be on holiday
at this point.

'Yes awful isn't it,' she typed at typical mum-pace, replying in the time it would have taken me to compose seven emails and a sonnet.

'Oh dear, they've got to her too,' I sighed.

When the online mob (and my mum) saw a black boy in a monkey hoody, they saw an offensive image. And I can understand why. Black people have a very uncomfortable relationship with the word 'monkey' – it's a loaded word that has been hurled around football stands and spat viciously across train carriages. When coming from ill-intentioned mouths, the word 'monkey' is hate speech. It carries with it a history of abuse – the type of abuse that no longer needs to be shouted across the street but can instead be woven tauntingly into the fabric of modern-day life.

Because of this, a significant number of people believed that the placement of a monkey hoody on a black child was H&M's way of quietly expressing their deep-seated racism. It didn't matter that the brand had proudly partnered with Beyoncé in 2013, or that the Sudanese supermodel Alek Wek had been an ambassador for the H&M Foundation for almost four years. The fact that they had recently featured Nicki Minaj, Kevin Hart and Naomi Campbell in their ad campaigns was irrelevant. After all, sharing in the influence of notable black faces doesn't grant you a get-out-of-bigotry-free card. So no, none of that came into it. Because H&M were racist. Apparently.

Wading through the posts it became clear to me that several people thought that H&M were provoking the black community for the purposes of publicity. As if one of the world's leading high-street juggernauts, with annual profits of more than $1 billion, suddenly had the urge to risk it all for a bit of notoriety.

But these weren't the only theories being punted by the self-appointed keyboard correspondents of Twitter and Facebook; many felt that the race issue at play was more about representation in the workplace. After all, if H&M had some black decision makers in their ranks somebody in the meeting room probably would have spoken up and said, 'Hey colonisers, how about we don't call the black boy a cool monkey?'

To be fair, all of these perspectives were plausible. And their respective spokespeople were being particularly persuasive from their Twitter accounts. So I continued to thumb my way through the receipt-roll of outraged posts, impressed by my generation's ability to intellectualise a pullover.

Because truth be told, all I saw was a cute kid in a hoody. An unremarkable and inoffensive hoody. A hoody that likened playful children to cheeky monkeys; a motif that I'd seen on kids' clothes a thousand times before. In my eyes, the boy modelling it just happened to be black.

Suddenly it bothered me that in a world where racism was already jumping off the page, we were going in search of it by reading between the lines. That we were being outraged by the faint whiffs of racism next door rather than attending to the almighty stench of it on our own welcome mat.

I was disappointed that this is where our outrage had ended up. On the stockroom floor of sodding H&M. Our powerful self-expression was being used to get an £8 hoody pulled from shelves.

'Are you just going to sit in here on your phone?' interrupted my fiancée, sticking her head around the door and redirecting my attention to the imminent outrage looming right in front of me. I looked up from the screen, remembering that I was 5,000 miles from home and suddenly realising that the sun had gone down.

'No,' I said, 'I'm gonna write an article about outrage.'

'The Currency of Outrage'*
Published in the *Guardian*, 25 January 2018

Everyone is offended by everything. It's exhausting. Keeping up with all the non-inclusive, misogynistic, racist, homophobic, transphobic, xenophobic, ageist, cultural appropriating, body-shaming propaganda that seems to litter the social media age. Apparently in 2018, almost anything is subject to the scrutiny of one marginalised eye or another. Being outraged allows you to take the moral high ground. It reaffirms your righteousness. It lets you say: 'I am offended and therefore I am principled.' It lets you jump on the bandwagon and pledge allegiance to the latest campaign on your timeline. It gives you a vehicle to add your name to the narrative. It proves that you are following current affairs, albeit from the comfortable vantage point of your Instagram feed. It allows you to place yourself on the virtuous side of the conversation. It says: 'I am woke.'

And for that reason, outrage has become currency.

* (The *Guardian* changed the name of the article to a clickbait-friendly title, see page xx).

Outrage was once reserved for the truly unjust. It was for civil rights activists and suffragettes. It has fought against police brutality, institutional racism, unequal pay, segregation and voting rights. Outrage gave a voice to the voiceless and forced society to take a long hard look in the mirror. It has challenged the status quo, prompted legislative review, torn down statues, conquered apartheid and abolished slavery. It gave birth to the life work of Malcolm X, Nelson Mandela, Simone de Beauvoir and Angela Davis. It ensured that the legacies of the Emmett Tills, Rodney Kings, Emily Davisons, Stephen Lawrences, Eric Garners, Marsha P. Johnsons and Mark Duggans were lasting. It gave us the words of Gloria Steinem, bell hooks, Bayard Rustin, Maya Angelou, Darcus Howe. It manifested itself in the riots of Watts, South Central, Brixton and Stonewall.

Outrage used to require more than a caption under a reposted picture. It required action and intent. It was the train that aimed to move protest towards progress. It was not a chess piece in a consumerist game. It was not an empty statement to endear oneself to the demographic of the day. It was warranted and validated.

There is still much to be outraged about in our postmodernist society; hate crimes against the LGBT community are increasing, the sale of slaves in Libya has persisted without intervention, the gender pay gap is so large that the ethnicity pay gap has been told to wait its turn, sexual predators are the kings of Hollywood, black men are given longer sentences than their white counterparts when convicted of the same crime in the

US and it is still illegal to be gay in more than seventy countries.

So what we're not going to do is channel our unwavering outrage towards the clumsy marketing techniques of H&M.

Writing this, I represent a 'triple jeopardy' intersection: a black, gay, woman. If we were playing Outrage Monopoly I would have properties on the high-ticket streets. My adult life has been punctuated by moments of outrage, both internalised and verbalised, against a world which has at times seemed intent on undermining and eroding my deviations from 'the norm'. Because of this, I am selective with my outrage. I do not have the luxury of campaigning against battery farming when my people are being shot in the back by LAPD.

But outrage is of course subjective. The British National Party are outraged by multiculturalism, leave-voters were outraged by Britain's open borders. Devout Christians are outraged by secular music. I do not share any of those concerns but this does not make them any less legitimate to each respective group. Outrage is therefore a currency with many different denominations, each of varied value in any given social marketplace.

If outrage is currency then think of your expression of outrage as an investment. It is emotionally draining to be truly outraged. It takes effort and energy to articulate the nuanced sentiments behind your indignation. It goes beyond simply 'taking offence'. You are outraged because you seek growth, change, evolution; a return on your investment. Smart investors do not

inject their finances blindly into every opportunity
that presents itself, yet we are now in a state of constant infuriation in response to any cause that picks
up enough momentum. Our outrage portfolios are a
mess and we aren't even tracking our profits and losses.
Outrage is no longer the mouthpiece of the activists, it
is the plaything of the commentators.

Last December social media was collectively
outraged by the bullying of Tennessee student Keaton
Jones. Celebrities rallied around the eleven-year-old,
clamouring to be louder and more supportive than
the next. The bullies were vehemently denounced and
Keaton was hailed as a superhero, all in response to a
seventy-second video. Everyone from Rihanna to Justin
Bieber was publicly incensed by the treatment of the
young teen. By the following Tuesday Keaton's family
had been exposed as Confederate-flag-wielding white
supremacists and the tide of outrage turned. In a case
study which epitomised the currency of outrage, the
Internet was quite literally looking for refunds. Words
of support were retracted and invitations to premieres
scrapped. Keaton went from hero to villain at the click
of a refresh button. By Thursday all was forgotten.

By becoming fickle and oversaturated, the value of
outrage is plummeting. In fact if you've got capital tied
up in outrage, I'd consider pulling out now before the
stock implodes completely.

It is said that if you stand for nothing then you will
fall for anything. But surely standing for everything
won't get you anywhere either. Martin Luther King Jr.
didn't hop from cause to cause. Sojourner Truth didn't

stray from her mission in favour of the latest headline-grabbing movement. And it is in that commitment to change, that unwavering belief in our outrage, where revolution is born. The Suffragette movement existed on both sides of a century. The Civil Rights Movement spanned over a decade. Even the London Riots of 2011 raged on for five days. Collective outrage was once so charged, so relentlessly sustained, that it acted as a catalyst for tangible progression.

These days, the lifespan of outrage rarely exceeds twenty-four hours or at least until our attention is diverted towards the next hot talking point. People are so intent on projecting a self-serving image of morality that they now piggyback any prominent cause that might help position themselves as ethical and compassionate. Publicists tell their clients to 'find a cause'. Columnists scramble for negative interpretations on which to base their think-pieces. Social media influencers can now find themselves engaging in three or four Twitter battles a week to prove that they are pro-choice, anti-racist, body-positive vegans.

And this is not to undermine the genuine endeavours of many twenty-first-century activists, nor is it intended to dismiss some causes as less worthy than others. It is simply to highlight this devaluing of outrage that occurs as a by-product of excessive uproar.

If we are all outraged all of the time, then outrage simply becomes the default setting. Nobody's outrage is given its rightful platform for any significant period of time because here comes another ill-thought-out ad campaign that misrepresents dog owners.

Excessive outrage derails movements by adding too many trains to the track. Black Lives Matter, but wait, polar bear lives also matter, and have you even stopped for a second to consider the real meaning behind Thanksgiving? By shouting about everything, we are in fact creating a deafening silence where outrage is without consequence. Politicians can avoid law reforms, newspapers can sidestep retractions, murderous police officers can evade prison sentences, safe in the knowledge that it will all blow over.

The currency of outrage is no longer worth its weight in gold. Traders are practically giving it away to anyone who will take it.

In 2017 the *British Medical Journal* published an article arguing that Peppa Pig was fostering an unrealistic image of the NHS. Seriously. A cartoon based around a talking farm animal was piling the pressure on the UK's doctors and nurses. It was a trending topic on Twitter for most of the day, people were outraged by the article's outrage which spawned yet more perplexing articles of faux outrage. But in that same week barely anyone heard the whispers about the Crown Prosecution Service's decision not to charge the five officers who allegedly contributed to the death of black musician Sean Rigg in police custody. There simply wasn't enough outrage to go round, so the fictional pig was granted the column inches.

Online outrage had us trying to #StopKony in 2012. *TIME* called it the most viral video of all time and there were estimates that half of the population's young adults had seen the campaign film *Kony 2012.*

But did we stop Kony? Who knows. We all lost interest and made way for Gangnam Style. But long before the hypersensitive, hashtag-hungry Internet Age, outrage existed – undistracted and unwavering. It was provocative and empowering. It threw itself in front of the king's horse and marched on Washington. It defined entire eras and rewrote laws with defiant, unrelenting, Underground-Railroad-building resilience. That's true outrage. Outrage doesn't sit on its sofa complaining about how Kim Kardashian culturally appropriated braids. It refuses to give up its seat on the bus in 1950s Alabama.

The day my article was published I sat on the edge of my bed and awaited the backlash. I was convinced that the few who could be bothered to read it would be horrified before they reached the end. Sure, my overprotective agents had censored what they could, because apparently 'you can't call Donald Trump a psycho', but still. I felt as though I was feeding myself to the lions.

My hot take on outrage was only going to trigger more outrage. The irony would be unbearable. I just knew it. How dare I use my university-educated, Western-living, media-personality privilege to undermine anyone's right to be pissed off? People had fought for my freedom to be selectively outraged and here I was dismissing new age activism. What if I was living a liberal fallacy, conditioned by my oppressors who had taught me to bite my tongue and not complain (then convinced me that it was my idea)? Shit, was I just a modern-day 'house negro', yelling at my cousins in the field to quit their whining? What if I'd gotten some facts wrong?* Or worse still, what if I sounded like a know-it-all? Nobody likes a know-it-all. Maybe it wasn't too late to get the article pulled? Surely I could just recall my emails and avoid the terrifying fallout, which had by now manifested itself in my mind so vividly I could smell the impending unemployment. 'The article just went up,' read the text from the press office. Ah crap. Here we go then…

I clicked the link, ready, I thought, for my public dragging. Up it popped: AS A BLACK, GAY WOMAN I HAVE TO BE SELECTIVE IN MY OUTRAGE. SO SHOULD YOU. One of the editors had stuck a provocative clickbait headline on my piece. This was it: I was dead meat. My first and last column. The world's shortest literary career ever. I would for ever be known as the radio DJ who thought she could play minority Top Trumps in order to police outrage. 'I'm going to be a pariah,' I thought, 'or worse still… I'm going to be Jan Moir.'

There are two moments in my life that ended up far better than I had initially feared. The first was when, aged eight, I cracked my head open on a sideboard while playing 'the floor is lava' and had to be rushed to A&E on a school night – six stitches later I was left with a pretty cool scar and a brilliant anecdote for future dinner parties.

The second moment was the day I realised that I wasn't the only one bored to death of outrage.

---

* Turns out the criticism of Peppa Pig in the *British Medical Journal* had been intended as a tongue-in-cheek article for their festive issue. Whoops.

'At last some sanity! This should be compulsory reading for Twitter users,' read one comment. 'Brilliant exposé of the whole loathsome "virtue signalling" tiresome know-nothings, desperate to find anything to take "offence" at,' added a second. 'Nail on head,' read another. God, this felt even better than 500 likes on a holiday snap. People were even sharing their own stories of misplaced outrage: 'This was the perspective I needed after almost being triggered this morning,' read one such Facebook post; 'I have reined in my social media outrage over the past year and it's been beneficial … Sometimes you have to let the bandwagon roll on by,' read another. I seemed to have stumbled into a refuge for like-minded voices seeking asylum from the social media battlefront.

It was the most-read opinion piece on the *Guardian* that day and only a handful of readers wanted my head impaled on a stick. ('How very sanctimonious of you to think you can tell people what to do and how to feel,' tweeted one unhappy customer. 'Why feel the need to state race, gender and sexuality before making a point as if that has some impact on its validity?' posted another in the comments section. 'Why do you think anybody cares what political categories you want to wear as badges? You have a big ego Dotty!' read another bad review.)

As the conversation around my article continued, I wondered what had happened to our outrage, that once-useful rebellion that now seemed so ineffective. Could we get it back, or were we doomed to a lifetime of hashtag movements and online petitions posted on Facebook?

Because, honestly, I wasn't sure I could take another fucking hashtag.

I wanted to unpack the phenomenon of modern-day outrage, the aimless social media posturing that had turned our feeds into cesspits of ill-feeling. How the hell had we ended up here? Raging and cancelling at will like self-righteous maniacs. And what had been the outcome of some of these crusades? We were engaging in the sport of outrage, but had anybody even been keeping score? I was determined to revisit some of these online draggings in an attempt to figure out what it had all been for.

So this book is for anyone who has been outraged, or suffered at the hands of it. For those of us who have been cancelled or orchestrated a cancelling. It is for anyone who cheered when a low life lost their job over an inappropriate tweet or resurfaced photo, and for those of us who were smart enough to wipe our own Twitter accounts clean.

Think of the following pages as an outrage intervention for anyone who has gotten high on indignation (and everyone who thinks they're already clean) because in this godforsaken age of Internet rage, uproar is one hell of a drug.

1

THE PROBLEM WITH RACHEL DOLEZAL

On 11 June 2015, a news item on a local cable network in Spokane, Washington featured an interview with a little-known NAACP* activist by the name of Rachel Dolezal.

The KXLY-TV interview is at first unremarkable. The unedited footage, which has since amassed almost 3 million views on YouTube, begins routinely with Dolezal (sporting a woefully misguided crimp hairstyle) answering a series of questions about some race-related hate crimes that she had reported to the police. She stands unassumingly on a downtown Spokane sidewalk, having been doorstepped by a reporter outside the Starbucks on West Main Avenue, just a short walk from the NAACP HQ.

'Do you think that the police department is trying hard enough to get to the bottom of who's terrorising you?' asks reporter Jeff Humphrey, standing off-camera. 'I'm not sure,' Rachel responds, with the assured smile of someone who is used to fielding media attention. 'When it comes to the formality of deciding what a hate crime is I really try to let the police make that decision.'

* National Association for the Advancement of Colored People.

But this line of enquiry actually has very little to do with the noose Rachel Dolezal claims was left hanging in the garden for her two black sons to find. It is in fact the clever probing of a crafty journalist who is biding time, waiting for the right moment to deliver his almighty sucker punch.

'Are you African American?' he asks her suddenly.

You've heard of a deer caught in headlights, well this was a deer caught in the tunnel of the Monaco Grand Prix. 'I don't... I don't understand the question,' she eventually stutters in a now infamous response for ever etched in meme history as an eternal source of second-hand embarrassment for anyone who dares watch it.

'Your parents, are they white?' the reporter persists, still standing out of shot so we can't quite see the photograph he is now holding up of a black man she posted on Facebook, claiming he was her father.

Unaware of the colossal shitstorm heading her way, Rachel Dolezal looks down at her feet and hastily walks off-camera, with the mother of all fallouts hot on her heels.

For over a decade, Rachel Dolezal, a white woman who still insists on the validity of her 'transracial' status, had successfully pulled off a cultural heist by pretending to be black. After divorcing her African American husband in 2005, she shed her own racial heritage and began meticulously creating an ethnic fiction that she claims to have yearned for most of her life. With wigs, weaves, civil rights activism, a bizarre backstory about being 'born in a tepee' and what appears to be a shedload of bottled bronzer, Rachel's watertight con would go undetected for years, securing her jobs and platforms in various black spaces across the Pacific Northwest.

She was appointed in an unpaid role as the regional president of the NAACP – America's 'oldest, largest and most widely recognized civil rights organization', created in 1909 to further the interests of oppressed and segregated black people across the United States. She taught race and culture studies in Eastern Washington University's Africana department while also acting as an adviser for the black student union. She worked as a columnist for her local paper the *Inlander* and, perhaps most significantly (for reasons that will become clear), she served as chair for the Office of the Police Ombudsman Commission in Spokane – a public body responsible for investigating complaints of misconduct by police officers.

When the mask eventually slipped on KXLY-TV she was immediately branded a 'race faker'. And within a week she was unemployed.

Less than ten hours after Jeff Humphrey's local scoop, the story had landed in the national press with Rachel Dolezal's parents (a white couple from Montana) wheeling out the family photos on NBC, CNN, ABC, CBS and Fox News as her dad told the world that his daughter 'was a blonde, blue-eyed, freckle-faced girl growing up'. Within a day she was making global headlines in what would become an era-defining moment of outrage.

I remember it well, scrolling through my Twitter feed one idle afternoon during my work-shy heyday, a lifetime before full-time employment and nursery pickups, and would excitedly click on articles with headlines like: CIVIL RIGHTS ACTIVIST RACHEL DOLEZAL IS 'PRETENDING TO

BE BLACK' SAY HER BIOLOGICAL PARENTS. My immediate reaction was one of stifled amusement. Yes, I admit
it; I was tickled by this strange woman I'd never heard
of and her ability to parade around as biracial in one of
America's most Caucasian cities. Her life seemed to be an
odd Ali G/Iggy Azalea mash-up event. To me, her disguise
was as absurd as Clark Kent managing to conceal himself
as Superman simply by removing his glasses and slipping
into a Lycra jumpsuit. After all, she wasn't just white: she
was Czech, Swedish and German. She was whiter than the
2016 Oscars.

In my eyes, Rachel Dolezal was a master of decep-
tion. She was Tom Ripley in the race-faking flesh. She'd
somehow managed to pull off the hoax of a lifetime using
little more than a lace-front wig and a tan. Her ability to
keep the ruse alive for as long as she did was nothing short
of impressive.

Sure, the online gatekeepers of acceptability were
screaming at me to take offence at this modern-day min-
strel show. And maybe I should have listened. But I didn't,
choosing (perhaps inappropriately) to see the funny side
instead.

'I'd happily take Rachel Dolezal in a swap for Raven-
Symoné,' I jokingly tweeted on the same day, referring to
the black actress who had recently rejected the label of
'African American' in an interview with Oprah Winfrey.

But I soon realised that the rest of the world wasn't
quite seeing the funny side. 'She's a con artist!' fumed
Montel Williams on CNN, before adding that he was
'offended by everything she has the nerve and the audacity to say'. 'I identify Rachel Dolezal as a lying, deluded

idiot,' wrote Piers Morgan (who is a far bigger threat to society than she will ever be, but more on that later) in one of his columns.

Here was a woman who only a day earlier had little to no profile outside of her own community, now being dragged through the thorny bushes of Twitter. The outrage towards her was both immediate and widespread, somehow managing to offend everyone from the neo-Nazis to the black academics, which in social terms is the equivalent of picking up an improbable 7–10 split in a game of bowling. She received death threats from the far right, who labelled her a 'race traitor' and an insult to her culture, with many even accusing her of 'creating white genocide', while the black opposition were branding her a 'cultural appropriator' and 'culture vulture' in blackface.

Contributing to the *Huffington Post*, the writer LisaMarie Rollins called it 'manipulation of race' and likened Dolezal to white supremacists for what she claims was a 'bending' of racial boundaries at the expense of black lives. Another commentator, Rebecca Carroll, called it 'apocalyptic white privilege on steroids' and accused Dolezal of having a 'colonization mentality'.

In the days that followed, Dolezal was taunted on NBC's *Late Night with Seth Meyers* and ridiculed on Comedy Central's satirical *Daily Show* with Jon Stewart. The lambasting was relentless. She even received a belated dressing down from the television psychologist Dr Phil two whole years later. 'You're not a victim in this,' he berated her in 2017.

The world had unanimously agreed that Rachel Dolezal was a raving lunatic who had to be cancelled like an

Amazon Prime subscription on day twenty-nine of the free thirty-day trial.

But to understand the outrage surrounding Rachel Dolezal, it is necessary to give it context, because all of this came at a time when the race dialogue in America was incredibly strained. The black community was still mourning the unpunished murders of Eric Garner, Michael Brown, Freddie Gray and Tamir Rice – unarmed black men, all killed at the hands of prejudiced police in the twelve months prior to Dolezalgate (not forgetting less-publicised black women like Tanisha Anderson, Yvette Smith and Miriam Carey, who were all killed in similar circumstances). Suffice to say, racial tensions in the United States were uncomfortably high and there was no shortage of super-villains for us to point our finger at. But while we were forgetting the names of those homicidal police officers, it was Rachel Dolezal's name we had chosen to etch in history.

When I decided to write this book, I was determined to speak to Rachel Dolezal. If I was going to look at outrage more closely, my first stop on the journey had to be someone who had lived through it. I wanted to learn what affect our outrage had had on her. Sure, we'd all moved on to our next moral crusade by now, but what had we left behind? For me, Rachel Dolezal was the car crash I couldn't help but slow down for with morbid curiosity. The kind that has you crawling at 8 mph on the off-chance that you might spot a bloody limb on the hard shoulder. So I figured I had nothing to lose by contacting her for a post-mortem.

I took a shot in the dark and fired off a speculative email through the contact page on her admittedly conspicuous website.

I attached the *Guardian* article I'd written and hit send. A day or so went by and the reply I never expected never came. I assumed my email had landed in some rarely monitored Gmail inbox, tossed alongside countless other unread punts from authors and journos. Until I woke up on Monday morning to find a carefully composed email in my inbox.

'Thank you for reaching out to me with such a refreshing approach to our current state of affairs in society,' she wrote, before pointing out that autocorrect had mistakenly changed the spelling of her surname to 'Doleful' in my email. 'It was somewhat poetic that you misspelled my name to mean a word associated with misery, because this whole experience of worldwide social shaming has indeed been a tormenting experience.'

I hurriedly wrote my apologetic response, mortified by the typo and still in disbelief that I was communicating with Rachel directly. I asked her whether she might be visiting the UK to promote the Netflix documentary *The Rachel Divide*, which was scheduled for release later that spring, hoping it might give us a chance to meet in person. But she said the production company wouldn't be paying for any tours and that her own finances had been crippled by her infamy. She told me that the level of outrage had 'paralysed' her 'economic situation' and that her book *In Full Color: Finding My Place in a Black and White World* hadn't sold enough copies to pay off the publication advance. So she was stuck in Spokane, 'braiding hair, applying for jobs and pushing the products on [her] website to keep the lights on'. I found it bizarre that she was offloading her financial baggage to me so soon and could only imagine what an absolute oversharer she must be on a first date, but I'd gotten this far and wasn't going to back down on account of her being an oddball.

So, owing to her apparent destitution and my aversion to connecting flights, we arranged a Skype call for the following Tuesday at 6 p.m. GMT, factoring in the seven-hour time difference between London and Washington. I sat at my dining table, carefully typing in her username while the washing machine whirred at an unnecessary decibel level, reiterating my belief that open-plan living is an acoustic hellscape that only serves a purpose if you are hard of hearing or Scandinavian. I paused my mid-wash cycle and connected the call, waiting for her to appear on screen with the apprehension of a mariachi band at a Trump rally. What if she really was the absolute psychopath the media had painted her out to be? Would I even recognise the signs of a pathological liar? And what would her hair look like? Would she be wearing the famous curly wig from 2015? Perhaps she'd thrown caution to the wind and gone full Rastafarian by now.

Before I could allow myself to get fully freaked out by a woman who PRETENDS TO BE BLACK, there she was, in what seemed like an instant, sitting against an ironically off-white wall in her living room, a scalp full of tight brown braids wrapped neatly in a knot above her head.

'Hey, how are you!' she said warmly, in a voice that was so familiar to me from the barrage of footage I'd seen of her since 2015 that it felt, rather weirdly, like I'd known her for years.

The hour that followed would leave me completely unsettled – and perhaps with more questions than I started with – but what I knew for sure was this: Rachel Dolezal's story is a cautionary tale, one that shows us everything that is wrong with modern outrage.

'If you could just cast your mind back to June 2015, which I'm sure isn't too hard to do,' I asked, 'when the story initially broke. Did you anticipate the level of outrage that was going to come your way?'

'No,' she began, with a weary half-smile that seemed part vulnerability, part exasperation at having told this story a bajillion times. 'When it kicked off I thought it was just gonna be local. I didn't think it would be national or international... I expected outrage,' she went on, 'because there's always been local outrage at everything I do. I mean, mostly by the white supremacists and white media here because it's uh...' She paused to recall one of the many stats she is armed with. 'It's like two per cent black here. So it's really majority white and very, um... very conservative, very Republican. And so a lot of my activism was met with opposition. I was kinda used to that. You know, everything that I did for the cause was countered or opposed. So that just like came with the turf...'

'And when you say "the cause", what are you referring to?' I asked.

'Everything I was doing at that moment was united in one purpose,' she said. 'I was the chair of the Police Ombudsman Commission for the city and in that role I was challenging police brutality not just locally but actually at the national level.' It sounded pretty impressive, especially to me, someone who had done little more than post a few #BlackLivesMatter tweets. Perhaps spotting the mild approval on my face, she upped the ante: 'I was collaborating with the Department of Justice to reboot the way that officers are trained, to reduce racial bias, racial profiling, shooting incidents, homicides, black ops, that kind of thing.' Suddenly she sounded like she was reeling off qualifications for a job I couldn't give her.

'I had actually just flown to Baltimore to support the protestors there against the homicide of Freddie Gray,' she continued. 'I was trying to learn some of their strategies and approaches because the cops here killed a black man in the jail.'

I had heard nothing about the latter incident and asked her to tell me more about this seemingly unreported case of police brutality in Spokane, but her two-year-old son had begun fussing off-camera. I was suddenly having to use my outdoor voice to compete with his shrieking. The interruption became so unbearable I may as well have left my bed sheets on their Tuesday night boil-wash just to compound the racket.

I flashed a pursed-lip smile, mum code for *I feel your pain but sort your shit out.*

'Hold on a second,' she said, disappearing out of view to tend to him.

And then she was back, looking more flustered than before but eager to pick up where we had left off.

She began, rather excitedly, telling me the detailed story of Lorenzo Hayes, a father of seven who had been killed at the hands of police in Spokane. 'The cops came and arrested him for violating a protection order, like thirteen white male cops threw him on the ground. He threw up and they held him down and he suffocated on his own vomit,' she explained with the fluency of a coached witness in a legal deposition. 'Nobody saw that video except for the people who were sworn to secrecy under, like, city code, right, which was me and the police officers,' she said, explaining that she'd been shown the highly confidential footage in her capacity as chair of the Police Ombudsman.

'So the chief of police basically called me in and was like, you know this is not a Black Lives Matter moment,' she continued. 'I was leading the #BlackLivesMatter movement here in Spokane – the marches, the protests. And so he said, "Don't talk to the media, don't tell anybody about this."'

She claims it was shortly after this ominous conversation, and while meeting with local activists in Baltimore, that she received an unsettling message. 'I got a phone call from a reporter who said there was a private investigator that the chief of police hired to go try and dig up dirt on me and shut down the police accountability commission,' she said (an allegation that that the chief of police has denied).

If this was a conspiracy theory cunningly concocted by Dolezal over the past few years, it was impressively detailed.

'I kind of expected that they were gonna try some kind of a smear campaign,' she went on. 'When they actually did it, they took down me and the two other commissioners who voted strongly for police accountability. This story broke on a Thursday and by Monday all three of us were removed. But nobody even noticed because everything was so like, *is she black or white?* It was like a big distraction.'

Ever the cynic, I checked this out after our call and it turns out that the Lorenzo Hayes part, at least, was entirely true. And his death had certainly been suspiciously under-reported, with only one article posted on the day of his passing (ironically by Jeff Humphrey, on KXLY, who would go on to break the Dolezal scandal four weeks later).

PRISONER DIES AFTER STRUGGLE WITH SPOKANE JAIL GUARDS[*]

SPOKANE, Wash. – A man suspected of violating a domestic violence protection order died at the Spokane County Jail Wednesday morning shortly after he was taken into custody.

Spokane police were dispatched to a home near Holy Family Hospital just before 6 a.m. after a caller said a couple were arguing and the man had hidden a rifle on the side of the duplex.

Lorenzo Hayes was arrested for violating a domestic violence no-contact order, but Hayes's cousin says it's the ex-girlfriend who came over and started the trouble.

Another local article posted three months after the incident then quietly revealed that the death had been ruled a homicide:

[*]'Prisoner dies after struggle with Spokane jail guards', Jeff Humphrey, KXLY, 13 May 2015.

RESTRAINED ARRESTEE CHOKED ON VOMIT, DIED IN
SPOKANE JAIL BOOKING AREA*

The Spokane County Medical Examiner's Office has
determined the death of a man in May in the Spokane
County Jail was a homicide.

Lorenzo Hayes, 37, died when he choked on vomit
while restrained in a prone position as a result of meth-
amphetamine toxicity, the Medical Examiner's Office
announced in a news release.

There is a video surveillance camera in the booking
area, and investigators have footage of the incident,
said Washington State Patrol Trooper Jeff Sevigney. The
video has not been released to the public.

Predictably there were no criminal charges against any
of the officers. No immediate suspensions, resignations,
consequences or compensation of any kind. Which is even
more telling when you learn that the killing of Lorenzo
Hayes was one of four inconspicuous deaths at the Spokane
County Jail in a period of three months. Inexplicably, this
troubling death toll didn't even make the local headlines.
Why was it, then, that Rachel Dolezal remained on national
news feeds for weeks? Was one woman's identity crisis really
more pressing than one of Washington's deadliest jails?

If there had indeed been a plot to bury the incident then
it had certainly gone to plan.

Here was a woman in good legal standing, with some
social stature at a local level, a degree of political sway
and a reputation for activism in the face of racial injustice,

---

* 'Restrained Arrestee Choked on Vomit, Died in Spokane Jail Booking Area', Nina Culver,
The Spokesman-Review, posted 1 Aug 2015

claiming that she had seen footage of police killing a black man. Wouldn't a bit of contrived outrage damage her credibility enough to extinguish any thoughts she may have had of inciting a police brutality race row? After all, what's a little character assassination between friends?

I couldn't be sure myself, but wondered whether Rachel thought her demise was entirely engineered to hide another issue.

'Oh yeah, absolutely,' she said. 'There's no way that somebody's personal identity can go from like a local issue to a global outrage without some engineering, without some organisation for leaking all that to the press, to the right channels.' She sat up like a flat-earther when they think they may have convinced you that the world is a two-dimensional disc. 'See, they had to create enough outrage to where they could remove me and those two other commissioners, shut that down and get me out of being like a threat to the police and the city government. They had to achieve that in a way that was unquestionable, that would prey on the sensibilities of the masses. Race is such an emotional topic. The rest is history.' She spoke without pausing for breath and left me feeling like I'd ended up on some deranged YouTuber's conspiracy channel.

Sensing perhaps that I needed respite, her toddler began squealing again, which forced her to rush off-camera and gave me a chance to process the complex machinations she'd just dumped in my lap. I wondered how a woman without the means to fund childcare could find the time to dream up such an elaborate plot if there wasn't at least some truth to it. I waited patiently for her to return to my screen and tell me more about this mind-boggling government ruse.

'It's not on some simple sound bite that I base my identity,' she said, coming back to the screen and having apparently decided to change the subject while she'd been seeing to her baby. 'You know, it's not just like, oh I'm black 'cause I just decided to wake up black one day.' She went on without pausing, almost as if giving someone a chance to speak meant giving them a chance to judge. 'Blackness to me is a consciousness. It's not a colour. It's an awareness. It's a state of mind. It's about fighting for justice and equity and being part of the family. Like fighting for the family, the original human family and not about, like, me being some white ally or saviour or some shit like that.'

As she continued to steamroller me with unsolicited race theory I grew concerned that she looked at blackness as some sort of club to which she could simply choose to subscribe. Why did she feel the need to 'join' the black race? Why couldn't she simply be an ally? This thing I'd found funny a few years ago suddenly started to feel slightly sinister.

She explained that she saw herself as a bridge between white allies and black fighters. 'Almost like, um, you know like a mixed-race person or something like that,' she said, as I leaned back at the Caucasity*. 'But, you know, to me that is problematic, terminology-wise.' She backtracked, reading my discomfort. 'It's not academically correct to say biracial because there's one human race,' she added. 'I just instinctively knew that black is beautiful and black is inspirational to me. Something about it just resonated with my soul like this is my original family. This is me. We actually all go back to a black mother.'

*Caucasian audacity

This is where I found myself exercising the patience I'd been encouraged to harness at Parentcraft. Instinctively recalling those mindfulness techniques you're taught to adopt as first-time parents so you don't end up screaming into a pillow after hour six of intermittent night feeds, I breathed in for three... two... one... and out again... mustering all the composure I needed to stop myself becoming visibly annoyed by a woman who seemed to think my ethnicity was a fashion statement.

But part of the problem with Rachel is that she doesn't seem to understand why there's a problem. In her 2017 memoir she even goes as far as likening her childhood to slavery. 'It wouldn't have been too much of a stretch to call me an indentured servant,' she wrote, claiming she was burdened with a 'dawn to dusk' workload of manual labour (or, as the rest of us call it, household chores). She elaborated on this tyrannical upbringing during our Skype call, accusing her parents of being 'abusive white supremacists' and believers in 'The Curse of Ham' — a disturbing interpretation from the book of Genesis, which asserts that all black people are born into servitude. Her long list of allegations also included a claim that her parents, Larry and Ruthanne, adopted four black children for financial gain before pushing them out of the house when they became teenagers and an insistence that she had been beaten by her parents when, aged five, she began to draw pictures of herself with brown crayons (something her parents have refuted for years). 'I think there's a demonstration of being irrational and being disconnected from reality,' Ruthanne had said in a CNN interview in 2015 when Rachel first threw them under the bus.

But Rachel's most damning testimony was reserved for her brother Joshua, who she tells me was the parents' 'favourite kid' – a man she claims sexually assaulted both her and her adopted sister throughout their childhoods.

I was at first unsure why Rachel felt the need to tell me all of this. Was she using it to justify her detachment from the family identity? Did she think she might mitigate some of the outrage by sharing a more sympathetic story? Or was she using me as some sort of freebie therapist?

She shared these deeply personal stories with me as though telling them for the first time (when really she has been spinning this yarn for years to anyone who would listen). According to Rachel, her brother Joshua (who has also published a memoir, FYI*) had been scheduled to stand trial for sexual-assault crimes in August 2015 and Rachel was apparently due to speak as a prosecution witness. This, she claims, was the reason her parents were complicit in the scandal. They wanted to protect Joshua, she says. 'He's the only one perpetuating their white bloodline,' she told me.

The charges against Joshua were ultimately dropped and he continues to refute Rachel's allegations, so I wondered whether she genuinely believed that the chief of police and her biological family had colluded to defame her character in this elaborate outrage plot. So I asked her: 'How many layers do you think there are to this conspiracy?'

'Well, see when the police's private investigator got to the parents, right, they were more than willing to cooperate with this organised takedown because they

* *Down From the Mountaintop: From Belief to Belonging*, Joshua Dolezal, 2014.

also had their own agenda,' she said. 'I think it was really more them that made it national. Because the case was in Colorado and they had to affect the case at a national level because we live in Washington state. Josh lives in Iowa, right; the jury trial is in Colorado. So they had to basically discredit me and make everybody believe I'm a liar so that my testimony wouldn't count. I was the tiebreaker between a he-said she-said. She said he did it, he said he didn't do it. And then here's me. I'm a community activist. I'm a professor. I'm a writer for two papers. I work for the city for no pay … That's a very credible witness.'

My head was spinning. The whole thing seemed ridiculous and plausible in equal measure. And Rachel's never-ending list of adversaries seemed to get even longer as she claimed competitors within the NAACP were also benefitting from her demise.

'Some of the local black communities saw this as an opportunity … They knew that there was an opportunity for anybody black who would support the city's position and help take me down. They would get promoted. And that's exactly what happened,' she said. 'There are people who are opportunists who will just seize a moment to throw somebody under the bus because it's good timing for them to get something out of it.'

I was curious about how much of the vitriol, if any, was strategic. Were people really exploiting Rachel's circumstances to get ahead? Or were these just the self-pitying ramblings of someone who had been through the mill? It was hard to tell. So I made a note to look into the motivations of feigning outrage before asking Rachel my next question.

'Did you think black people would be on your side?'

'Well...' She paused, as though the question was one she hadn't contemplated before. 'I don't know that I really had time to set any expectations. I guess I really hoped there would be, maybe in the academic sector, some more support, because it's not a stretch for academics to realise that race is a social construct. You can't lie about a lie anyways.'

This idea of lying about a lie, although conceptually insightful, wasn't of her own making. It was a theory from an article I'd already read about her in *The New Yorker* back in 2015. The comment piece 'Black Like Her' by Jelani Cobb claimed that in truth 'Dolezal has been dressed precisely as we all are, in a fictive garb of race whose determinations are as arbitrary as they are damaging. This doesn't mean that Dolezal wasn't lying about who she is. It means that she was lying about a lie.'*

But I'm not writing this book to debate the nuances of race or to determine whether or not Rachel Dolezal is a basket case. What interested me in articles like Jelani Cobb's was the practice, not the theory, because although not supportive of Dolezal, his analysis of her behaviour did not rush to judgement either.

According to Rachel, scattered voices of support for her did exist, but the mainstream media was simply silencing them. 'I think the white media only wants one black response. And they want that to be against me so that they can keep me from returning to the work that I was doing,' she said. 'I did get a lot of support privately but nobody wants to do that publicly,' she went on. 'The media fed on

* 'Black Like Her', Jelani Cobb, *The New Yorker*, 15 June 2015.

the outrage. They fed on the opposition. The few people who were brave enough to support me just got censored. Their interviews got cut. A lot of people who did media interviews, they never had them aired.'

I thought for a moment and realised I couldn't actually remember many people who had openly vouched for Rachel Dolezal. There'd been Whoopi Goldberg, who said, 'If she wants to be black she can be black,' and Rihanna, who had called her 'a hero' in an interview with *Vanity Fair*, but these scarce exceptions aside, there were few voices stemming the tide of outrage. So maybe Rachel was right. Maybe the coverage had been engineered to create a villain. But if that were the case, just how much of the backlash had been curated by the media?

At least by speaking to Rachel I could bypass any press agendas. Through the magic of WiFi we were face to face, without the outside influence of newspaper editors or television producers. But I still didn't know what the hell to make of it all. I mean, this was the woman who had referred to herself as a 'Black-Is-Beautiful, Black liberation movement, fully conscious, woke soul sista' in her book, so you have to understand I was battling with an ongoing element of crazy.

I needed to know if she at least held herself partly accountable. 'Why do you think there was so much outrage?' I asked.

She sighed.

'Well… two things,' she said. 'On one side of the colour line white people reacted so vehemently because I was made into an example of what you should not do, like a line you should not cross. You stay in your place, you keep [in] your lane as a white ally only, that's the only thing acceptable, you do just a little bit, you don't go too far. You don't put a hundred on ten, as they say. You don't give up your whiteness. And then from the white liberals I feel like some of them were pissed off because I went further than they would ever go and that made them kinda look weak and lazy or like they didn't do as much. Then I think for the white supremacists that's pretty obvious; my kids are black, all the causes I fight for are exactly against everything they stand for, you know, the way I do my hair – I'm a braider, I always do braids, you know, weaves and stuff – not just for me but 99 per cent of it is for other people. I think in the black community though, the outrage was because there was so much pain. And because I reminded people of pain I was branded as the face of white privilege, to the point where it was acceptable for anybody and everybody to bash me.'

She also thought there was a lot of bitterness on a colourism level, a perspective she believes hasn't been spoken about enough. 'Most of the anger came from darker black women who were hurt on that colourism level, all the way back to the plantation era when if you were lighter you were better and you could work in the house instead of the field and you'd get paid more,' she said. I considered telling her that she might be digging a bigger hole for herself with this, but instead handed her a shovel by nodding intently. 'I think for mixed girls or lighter-skinned girls, it was an opportunity for them to prove their blackness by throwing me under the bus. If you could be blacker than Rachel or diss Rachel, then you were proving your loyalty to the darker sisters. And even for some men to prove that they really love black women, like dark-skin black women, if they threw me under the bus and said, "I'd never date her, she's fucked up," or whatever, then that like elevated or made the other sisters feel better.'

'So people were using your story to construct their own allegiances?' I asked. 'Yeah exactly,' she replied with an emphatic nod.

Much of the outrage that engulfed Rachel Dolezal was, however, based on the idea of 'cultural appropriation' – a phrase that wasn't actually added to the *Oxford English Dictionary* until 2017 (almost two years after it punctuated every other think piece on Dolezalgate), defining it as 'the unacknowledged or inappropriate adoption of the practices, customs, or aesthetics of one social or ethnic group by members of another (typically dominant) community or society'. So for many of Rachel's critics, this ethnic performance wasn't just some harmless self-identification; she was in fact commandeering the black narrative, breaching black spaces and imposing upon opportunities designed for people of colour. In perhaps the truest embodiment of colonialism she was effectively trying to surpass blacks at being black. But just six days after she was outed on local television, a far more heinous race crime occurred 2,000 miles away in South Carolina.

On 17 June 2015 Dylann Roof entered the Emmanuel African Methodist Episcopal Church in Charleston, South Carolina and murdered nine black people during Bible study. In the days and weeks that followed, it was the deluded race faker from Spokane who grew in notoriety, while the white supremacist on a killing spree seemed to slowly slip off our outrage radars. Were we perhaps being steered by news feeds that saw more mileage in a white woman impersonating black people than in a white man slaughtering them?

'I was looking at timelines and I didn't realise that your story ran almost parallel to the Charleston shooting,' I said. 'Were you surprised that you were still making headlines when something like this happened?'

'No I wasn't surprised... I think that's the culture we're living in. It could have been Kim Kardashian who took over the news when Dylann Roof happened. It could have been anybody. Because that's where we're at in society. We're confused about the level of importance of an issue. And we're also eating garbage when it comes to information. We're confusing sound bites with facts and rumours with actual intel. I wasn't surprised. I was disappointed that yet again people are focusing on something that should have never been an issue. Of course we should be caring about real issues of justice and public safety; I've never committed a crime.' She paused in what seemed to be a rare moment of genuine self-reflection. 'People feel like I committed a social crime, though.'

'It was a weird time,' she went on. 'Because Caitlyn Jenner's story just came out, then me, then Dylann Roof and a lot of people were picking which topic they wanted to weigh in on. Is it transracial and transgender as these buzzwords or is it race and justice? If we had more Rachel Dolezals would Dylann Roof be here? I think people were just, like, mixing all that stuff up.'

For years I'd wondered what had become of Rachel Dolezal, a woman whose punishment never quite felt like it fit the crime. I tried to get a sense of what was left of her, looking over her shoulder into her house for clues and noticing a distinct lack of, well, anything. Her walls were sparse, the natural light was wanting. So I just asked. 'What is life like for you now?'

'It's hard,' she said, describing the absence of family and friends. She told me that every job application she'd made since then had either been turned down or ignored. 'I couldn't even get an interview in 2015 or 2016,' she said. So at the end of 2016 she changed her legal name – 'to at least get my resumé seen and not just thrown in the trash' – an ambitious exercise in damage control that saw her boldly rebrand to 'Nkechi', a Nigerian moniker meaning 'Gift of God'. The Igbo name change was of course met with clowning en masse: 'If Rachel Dolezal can be Nkechi Diallo, can I identify as a white girl called Elizabeth at airport security?' wrote Nishaat Ismail in the *Independent*.

'Right now I don't have rent for April,' she said. I squirmed in my seat. Was she priming me to make a charitable donation to her bank account, I wondered? I couldn't help but feel a bit sorry for her. But not enough to become her sponsor. 'I might have to leave America,' she went on. 'I want to be in a society where I can work to undo white supremacy ... I don't want to have to braid hair for the rest of my life.'

'You must really feel black now,' I said.

'Well, I guess that's the joke,' she sighed. 'It's easy to say, but at the same time I don't feel more black, because I lost my community. I already exiled myself from whiteness. I don't have a white family. I don't have a white community. Nobody white likes me. So now I just don't have anybody. I don't know that I feel really black. I just feel really rejected.'

As much as I had begun to pity Rachel, there was a stubbornness about her that made me wonder whether she needed my sympathy at all. After all, in a world where everyone is apologising for everything, she had never shown even a glimpse of remorse. I was curious as to why she'd never said sorry to the people she'd offended. It seemed a strange act of defiance given the onslaught. Even if insincere, saying sorry would have been an easier way out.

Did she feel like she owed anyone an apology?

'Like an apology for what? For me, to apologise would be suicide,' she said. 'I can't go back to being twelve years old in that oppressed household trying to tell myself I'm white,' she added. 'I'm forty years old, I can't go back to a less-evolved state of my life … That to me is death. That's not living.'

'Besides,' she added, 'I don't think anything I say can make a difference. I don't think anything I say is gonna be heard by most of the people who are outraged, because outrage is like a drug. Somebody would have to go into rehab and not be outraged any more to actually hear what I have to say.' Ironically, the woman with the presumed personality disorder was claiming it was everyone else who needed treatment. But she had a point. I wasn't sure if we were ever truly outraged by Rachel or whether she had just helped us to scratch an itch; that hankering for moral superiority that had made outrage junkies out of us all.

'A lot of people are just gonna use me as a meme or as a comedy skit or as an example of what not to do,' she added.

To me, Rachel's story was the perfect example of modern outrage. It had private scandal, public humiliation, hidden agendas, performative social posturing; it was a Shakespearean play for the Facebook generation. It even had the tragic irony of Rachel being someone who had brandished race-based outrage and was now finding herself on the receiving end of it. So had she changed her mind about the power of outrage now that it was directed at her?

'Outrage is a tool, it can be used for good, it can be used for evil,' she said. 'It can be used to support the right thing, it can be used to support the wrong thing. It's just a tool, like the Internet. The Internet is good if we're educating ourselves, but it can also be a place where people hack and scam and do all kinds of criminal shit online. Outrage is like a hot potato: you want to pass it into the right hands at the right time.'

A month after our call, Rachel's Netflix documentary landed on the global streaming service. I emailed her in the hope of catching up again but received no response. I assumed she was busy dealing with the renewed interest in her story, possibly even capitalising on her return to the spotlight. Maybe this would be the light at the end of the tunnel for her, I thought.

Turns out that light was a train hurtling towards her at full speed. A few weeks later news emerged that Rachel Dolezal had been arrested on felony charges of welfare fraud, perjury and falsifying records for public assistance. Maybe she was a massive con artist after all. Or perhaps she'd been driven to desperate measures.

As I scrolled through pages of news reports on Rachel's arrest, wondering whether I'd been taken in by a deceptive or mentally ill storyteller, I asked myself whether anyone had gained anything from this whole thing. We hadn't dented the prevalence of racism. This hadn't been some watershed moment in the fight against cultural appropriation. So what was in it for us? What was the rationale behind our merciless takedown of this woman we'd never met? In a country where more than 10 million individuals changed their racial self-identification between 2000 and 2010 (yes, according to a study by the US Census Bureau alongside the University of Minnesota, thousands of Americans are doing the race hokey-cokey every single day), why were we so hung up on this one?

What could motivate people from all over the world to unanimously agree on an ambush? And what did it take to galvanise entire communities in the name of outrage? I wondered then, what exactly went into making a mob and did we even realise when we were part of one?

2

MAKING A MOB

I admit I had indulged in some Dolezal jibing myself. It was hard not to. I'd slipped her name into my radio show's annual send-up of that year's defining moments and, in all fairness, she was in equally ludicrous company. I mean, this was the year that gave us the godawful man-bun trend, the 'dab' and that *white and gold... no wait, it's blue and black* dress. There was no way Rachel Dolezal wouldn't be held accountable for her contribution to the circus.

'In the year that served up *Fifty Shades of Grey*,' I'd said, 'a no-stars-out-of-ten, chunder-stain of a movie that made us question whether sadomasochism might extend to ripping our own eyeballs out, there was also Rachel Dolezal looking for her perfect shade of brown. A decision I assume she made using a Dulux colour chart from B&Q...'

All in all I'd been pretty pleased with myself in the way wisecracking twats often are when we come up with something vaguely funny at somebody else's expense. But now that I'd spoken to her and seen some of the lasting effects of unrelenting persecution, I was feeling uncomfortable with the part I'd played in it all.

I tried to convince myself that my flogging of Rachel
had been in jest rather than outrage, so surely I couldn't be
classed as part of the mob. But whether I dared to admit
it or not, I had deliberately contributed to the noise by
revelling in her vilification. The whole thing was beginning
to feel regrettable. I suddenly realised that what I had mistakenly dismissed as indigestion was in fact the unfamiliar
pangs of guilt.

Sure, her ability to pick and choose her racial identity
is white privilege 101. But it's also pretty apparent that
there was no inherent malevolence in her actions. So what
had it all been for? Why had I jumped on the Dolezal bandwagon? In fact, why had any of us? Yes, we're taught that
injustice anywhere is a threat to justice everywhere, but
was this peculiar woman from Spokane really unpicking
the seams of humanity? What did we really stand to gain
by dragging a woman whose life choices had little, if any,
direct bearing on ours?

I wanted to know what was motivating us to assemble
into angry mobs online. What was it that had us foaming
at the mouth over the flimsiest of transgressions? It was
all I could think about. I was lurking on the Internet at all
hours of the day, waiting for something to kick off so I could
psychoanalyse the swarm. My interest in the mechanics
of outrage was taking on a life of its own. I hovered over
heated threads and contentious headlines, anticipating the
next big pile-on.

Alan Sugar posted a racist tweet about the Senegalese
World Cup squad and got torn another geriatric arse-
hole by the Twitter militia. A few weeks later Scarlett
Johansson, a white cisgender actor who had previously

been called out for playing the role of a Japanese cyborg, was cast in the role of a transgender man for a film called *Rub & Tug* – an apparent abomination that wokesters were branding 'trans-erasure'. She withdrew from the film just in time for us to shift our outrage to TV chef Jamie Oliver, who was being accused of cultural appropriation for his shakiest invention yet: jerk rice (we'll dive into that travesty later).

What began as a few minutes of Facebook snooping a couple of times a day was quickly turning into a full-time obsession. I was scrolling for hours at a time with two-minute toilet breaks, desperate not to miss a thing. It was as exhausting as it was thrilling, so on an unusually quiet afternoon, when Angry Twitter seemed to be having a day off, I decided to disengage and watch sitcom bloopers on YouTube instead.

Apparently YouTube had a better idea.

'How Morally Outraged Are You?' read the title of the recommended video (evidently, if you spend eighteen nights in a row watching outrage uploads, YouTube automatically assumes you have no other interests). I scrolled past the video because online algorithms aren't the boss of me, then scrolled back up to it and pressed play, because who am I kidding?

It was a brief discourse on our moral behaviour by an Ivy League professor called Molly Crockett, a neuroscientist who has spent years studying the patterns of human decision-making. The four-minute clip shows her (looking like one of those carefree white ladies who shop at Nordstrom) in a messy bun and chiffon blazer, eloquently summarising the social and moral benefits of expressed outrage. When the video ended, four more Molly Crockett talks popped up for me to watch. 'How Social Media Makes us Angry all the Time', 'Why Your Brain Loves Feeling Outraged', 'Moral Outrage in the Digital Age' and 'Culture and its Discontents: Outrage Activism'. She'd covered a lot of ground. Think of her, if you will, as the Taylor Swift of neuroscience.

I'd already made my own assumptions about the social perks of being loudly and visibly outraged in cyberspace. And I figured the collective pursuit of these perks was the driving force behind the formation of the mob. So I spent the next few days in a Molly Crockett rabbit hole, gorging on her theories for breakfast, lunch and dinner as she explained why we are so motivated to broadcast our expressions of disapproval online. Her ideas were easy to follow in a way that probably made Internet trolls with names like Apocalypse_439 think they too could be neuroscientists. I clicked on everything I could find, jotting down her snazzy sound bites so I could explore them further. Theories like: 'Outrage expression provides reputational rewards' (which she writes in her landmark thesis, 'Moral Outrage in the Digital Age'.*) *Reputational rewards*, I thought, *sounds like something you collect on a supermarket loyalty card at Morals2Go*. But it's a clever concept, one that succinctly categorised what I had begun to suspect might lie behind a lot of modern outrage.

'Online social networks massively amplify the reputational benefits of outrage expression,' she continues. 'While offline punishment signals your virtue only

* 'Moral Outrage in the Digital Age', M. J. Crockett, *Nature*, 18 September 2017.

to whoever might be watching, doing so online instantly advertises your character to your entire social network and beyond.' A cartoon lightbulb popped up above my head. This is exactly what I had been trying to articulate in my article when I wrote that outrage 'reaffirms your right-eousness'. Were we just using these online expressions of grievance to be self-congratulatory? Collecting moral Brownie points by pointing out even the slightest of improprieties?

What Molly suggests is that online outrage comes with the promise of character-enhancing advantages and we engage in moral warfare as a way of cashing in on these personal benefits. So our digital fits of rage aren't neces-sarily coming from a place of genuine concern; they might just be manifestations of our own vanity, a prop to boost our performance on the world's biggest stage. Of course! Why intervene during a racial attack on a flight when you can quietly record the footage from three rows away and broadcast your outrage to the whole matrix?

Shame a racist in person and you can ruin him for a day, but shame him online and you can dine out on it for life.

I wondered then whether we were all caught up in the moral theatrics of social media, condemning things in order to paint ourselves in the best possible light. Just as we put filters on our selfies to make them more flattering, isn't it feasible that we might exaggerate our values to hide our own moral blemishes? In an online landscape that encourages us to show off our best angles, it seemed a likely motivation behind fictive outrage.

Where outrage once served an evolutionary purpose, reshaping society and moving us from the dark ages of the 1950s into the slightly more progressive 1990s, it now seemed to have a more conceited function. I mean, it used to be our way of holding a mirror up to mankind and saying, 'Look at yourself!' but it now seemed to be an opportunity for us to hold a mirror up to ourselves and say, 'Look at me!'

We spend day and night grooming the way we are regarded by others, forging digital identities that are well read and better travelled. We compose finely tuned and heavily edited versions of ourselves so that everyone knows we have great cushions, bake bread on Sundays and totally care about refugees. Simulating outrage would certainly further this calculated pursuit of the 'exemplary me'; a deliberately designed prototype of who we wish we were. Faux rage is really no different to posing for a picture next to a fancy car that you don't own. It's aspirational. It puts us on moral high ground and we all like the way we look from up there.

Twitter and Facebook are megaphones for the self-absorbed. Convinced that everyone is listening (when in truth two thirds of the population have never ventured onto a 'timeline' in their lives), we find ourselves tirelessly crafting posts in the hope of creating a faultless feed. And nothing boosts our online stock quite like a widely shared post. Maybe you've experienced it. You tweet something clever, expecting a dozen or so retweets from your close circle of friends, associates and maybe Carol at work who reposts everything. You lock your phone and reheat last night's bolognese without giving your tweet a second thought. You check your phone an hour later and your notifications are on fire. Turns out everybody else thought your tweet was clever too. Thirty retweets, sixty retweets, 120 retweets. It multiplies every time you excitedly refresh the page. Before you know it, your tweet has gone double platinum and you're preparing your thank-you speech. It's a fucking rush. Or what Molly Crockett refers to as 'a pattern of reinforcement' that is 'well known to promote habit formation'.

This is often the driving mechanic behind viral outrage: that perfect storm of opportunity and engagement where entire populations weigh in on some controversy in the hope that their post will be the one that gets traction. The social-media-savvy collect likes and retweets like they're gold rings on Sonic the Hedgehog and will say anything if they think it might capture the consensus.

So is outrage merely an opportunity for us to flex our integrity in cyber-space?

Not everyone who posts furiously about the latest political scandal or social injustice is doing so from a place of genuine outrage. Quite often these moments of communal uproar are used as an opening, a chance to be the Twitter user who summed up the public point of view with one brilliant tweet.

We have all been guilty of it; drafting the perfect post to eloquently offer an opinion that nobody asked for. Dressing up our personal bias in a technicolour dreamcoat of decency and good intention. Could it be that we are all just virtue signalling?

Now when I say virtue signalling, I'm not talking about the bearable kind paraded around by eco-mums with their reusable upcycled tote bags from Planet Organic or Instagram dads who want a standing ovation for putting their daughter's hair in a ponytail. That's entry level. When it comes to staged outrage I'm talking about insufferable, self-righteous, vomit-inducing virtue signalling. The kind that convinces narcissistic do-gooders to film themselves feeding the homeless. Those charitable-on-camera types. The boastfully benevolent who flaunt their humanitarian values, not from a position of altruism but simply to satisfy their self-adulation.

Thanks to the Internet we can now virtue signal at fibre-optic speeds, disguising our ostentatious self-regard with politically charged posts, constructing saintly versions of ourselves that in truth exist solely online. And according to academics like Crockett, outrage is often part of this public performance. 'The ease of piling on raises the intriguing possibility that in online settings, people may express moral outrage without actually experiencing the degree of outrage their behavior implies,' Molly explains.

And of course there is no easier place to pile on than Twitter, where virtue signalling and simulated outrage go hand in hand, like child stars and rehab. Twitter can, in a day, expose you to more moral contraventions than you could ever witness over a year in your everyday life. On a single morning spent scrolling through Twitter you might encounter government corruption, inhumane detention centres, genocide and a mass shooting, all before you've even wiped the crust out of your eyes. It creates a moral tension that is almost impossible to ignore, with a 'post and share' model that implores you to engage and rewards you with approval.

'Social media apps streamline triggering stimuli and available responses into a heavily designed "stimulus-response-outcome" architecture that is consistent across situations,' writes Crockett, using her Yale University words. 'And just as a habitual snacker eats without feeling hungry, a habitual online shamer might express outrage without actually feeling outraged,' she continues, this time with an analogy fit for any IQ. What Molly is getting at here is that many of us are willing to simulate negative responses for the sake of engagement, even when these responses don't actually represent how we feel. So we sit on the sidelines of social media, anticipating any signs of a takedown, ready to flaunt our moral dexterity at the expense of Twitter's latest exile.

Or maybe I'm being entirely too harsh. Because we are by no means deliberately deceptive with our performative virtuosity. I doubt that we're all sitting at our desks with popularity projection charts, making calculated choices about when to get riled up online and how it might benefit us (unless, of course, you're a politician). So behind all the staged outrage, we mean well.

After all, loudly opposing the Trump administration's family separation policy from the comfort of your four-bedroom semi in Tunbridge Wells doesn't make you a bad person. It signifies, with minimal effort, that you're one of the good ones.

And members of a mob aren't necessarily in it for the narcissism alone.

OK, Molly's characterisation of modern egocentric ragers had provided a fitting starting point for my exploration of the mob, but it was by no means a definitive e-fit of what the culprits looked like. Because the truth is, modern outrage can look like you or me or your free-spirited Pilates instructor called Juniper. Sure, many of us will fit into Molly's neatly compartmentalised ideas about the mechanics of outrage, but there are just as many of us that won't. Some people feign outrage out of boredom, not narcissism. Others assemble into angry groups for camaraderie, not conflict. Then there are enigmatic mobs like Extinction Rebellion (where political protest meets bizarre street theatre), a group of eco-warriors who seem to have fetishised arrest in the name of climate change. It would be impossible to sort us all into definitive lists under tidy little columns.

And while outrage certainly has reputational rewards for the individual, it might also have cooperative rewards for the many.

It would seem that we love nothing more than to join the outrage conga line and revel in some good old-fashioned communal shaming. We have probably all at some point participated in some mass dragging, throwing in our two-pence-worth in the group shaming of some poor sod who just wanted a quiet life.

Outrage spreads with relative ease as we are, by nature, creatures of imitation, taking social cues from the behaviour of those around us. There is no better demonstration of this than on the Internet, where we use social media to follow the people we like, admire or enjoy engaging with. These customised communities lead to a heavily curated online experience, reflecting our own likes, morals and belief systems back at us. So while we might think our online feeds bear some true likeness to the world we live in, they are in fact a series of echo chambers that have created the illusion of tribalism and sorted us into online peer groups that fall in line with each other's perspectives.

And it seems as though this is how mob outrage is gathering momentum.

Take Rachel Dolezal, for instance. I, like many of us, had delighted in the pantomime of it all. But I still question whether any of us would have had the individual courage to confront her if she was just a local weirdo who lived on our street rather than a global hate figure already being judged online. After all, it's the crowd that often gives us our courage. You've seen it yourself a thousand times, that basic herd mentality that incites football hooligans, mobilises street gangs, convinces you to park on a yellow line because other cars have done it.

I think of this as 'the Choir Effect' and I'll tell you why. I spent a year in my school choir despite having the vocal ability of a tone-deaf house cat. Not a whiff of talent even on my best day. None. Not even a fraction. Yet there I was, on the third row with the altos, moving my lips but making absolutely no sound. I got away with this for an entire school year while enjoying all the benefits of the choir: I got to leave maths early for rehearsal, I got to hang out with Robin, our jaunty music teacher who let us call her by her first name; I even bowed on stage when we got a standing ovation at the Christmas assembly. But what has me lip-syncing to 'Oh Little Town of Bethlehem' got to do with outrage, I hear you cry. Well, everything. Just like my trusting Year 7 choir, outrage in numbers allows you to stand with the mob without actually contributing to the cause. It affords you the freedom to bask in the moment while never having to stand alone in the spotlight. You reap the rewards while escaping the scrutiny.

How many of us would be up for singing solo on a grand stage? Not many, I assume. The anxiety of public speaking is such a threat to our confidence that even the most

accomplished communicators get sweaty palms before a
work presentation. But the idea of being an imperceptible
voice in a choir? Now *that* doesn't seem so bad. And this
ability to hide while being seen is exactly how the Choir
Effect manifests itself in matters of outrage.

'Shaming a stranger on a deserted street is far riskier
than joining a Twitter mob of thousands,' writes Molly,
who found that the chances of backlash were lower when
we broadcast our disapproval to like-minded peers. So
we announce our damning judgements to our own social
circles, knowing that we are doing so from a position of
security. And I was beginning to realise that these feedback
loops were creating a collective conscience, compelling us
to act in unison and weaving the very fabric of mobocracy.

I thought back to what Rachel Dolezal had said to me
about the baying mob she encountered in 2015. She was
certain that the prominent voices within the pack had been
'angry black women' and I must admit this claim agitated
me. Having seen rotten tomatoes pelted at her from all
corners of the Internet, I resented the belief that the
outraged had been disproportionately black or female.

'There was just one black woman in the whole bunch
of people shouting,' Rachel said, singling out what she
believed to be the only black, female voice of support
among all the others. This was Dr Ann Morning, a professor of sociology whose work focuses on the concept of
race. Dr Morning had spoken publicly about the Dolezal
scandal and had been one of the few advocates for Rachel
with long reads like 'Kaleidoscope: Contested identities
and new forms of race membership', an essay published
in the academic journal *Ethnic and Racial Studies*, and 'It's

Impossible to Lie About Your Race', an article for the *Huffington Post*, in which she wrote that 'the common framing of the Dolezal case – as a matter of lying versus the truth – is the wrong one. Dolezal doesn't have a "true" race any more than she has a "true" astrological identity.'

I wondered then if Dr Morning would agree with Rachel's description of the mob. So I looked her up and after spending two hours searching for a free download link to her 'Kaleidoscope' thesis on the dark web, I eventually gave up and paid thirty-two quid for it on an official website for academic papers. The essay takes issue with society's rigid framing of race and, in light of this, questions whether there was ever a need for the backlash against Rachel Dolezal. In an attempt to understand some of these alternative perspectives that, if applied, might have saved Rachel from eternal damnation, I asked Dr Morning if she would share some more of her insights with me.

A few weeks later, we were exchanging emails at a rate that I can only assume was an absolute nuisance to her – though she was always perfectly accommodating. 'Sure!' or 'Wonderful!' she would write, in a way that made me imagine she was one of those Americans who welcome new families to the neighbourhood with baskets of muffins. Ann Morning was a fountain of data, the *phone-a-friend* who would catapult you to seven figures on *Who Wants to be a Millionaire*. It was Ann who told me the stunning fact that nearly 10 million individuals changed their racial self-identification between the 2000 and 2010 US censuses. So I asked whether she could offer her discernment on why we ignored the other 9,999,999 instances of race reversal, yet found Rachel's story so triggering.

'For me, that's the most interesting question of all!' she said. 'As a sociologist, it is quite uninteresting that a random person in Spokane has a racial identity that is at odds with our social customs. Instead, what is truly fascinating is why millions of people would take a passionate interest in that lone, unknown person.'

I had no idea why the mob had descended on this particular story. It now seemed so arbitrary. But Ann believed it was a sign of the times. 'It reminds us how deeply Americans believe that race is an essential, innate, fixed fact about human bodies. As much as some social and biological scientists have tried over the last half-century to disabuse people of that notion, Ms Dolezal's case shows us that it remains with us in spades,' she explained. 'People are not just shocked that an ostensibly white woman would call herself black, as if she had called a cat a dog, obscuring a clear-cut truth, but they are outraged about it, and that is what's so telling.

'I think there are multiple moral scripts at work here,' she continued (citing Rogers Brubaker's book *Trans* for its exploration of the roots of the Dolezal affair). 'There are transgender people who think her so-called "transracial" identity makes a mockery of their own; there are black people who place her squarely in the long tradition of whites appropriating black cultural forms; there are those who are disturbed by any kind of "trans" identity that seems to break with supposedly "natural" social roles. But if I had to put money on it, I would guess that none of these would have been enough on their own, or even together, to create the media firestorm; it's not really credible that the US public would rise up en masse to defend blackness.

I believe instead that Dolezal tapped into long-simmering anger on the part of whites about what they perceive as illegitimate uses of racial classification, especially affirmative action.'

For Ann, this was largely a consequence of Middle America's view that blackness had somehow become advantageous: 'We saw in the 2016 presidential election and since, how powerful white racial resentment is. And I believe that what mainly fuelled anger about Dolezal was the belief that she claimed a black identity in order to get material benefits – as if being black meant manna from heaven! In the US of all places.'

But did she agree with Rachel's profile of the 'angry black woman' being the loudest voice in the crowd of rage?

'I'm not sure that's the case,' she wrote back. 'We social scientists haven't yet taken careful empirical measure of what went on. Perhaps black women were more likely than others to vocalize, say on social media, what they thought about this case, but I'm not sure they made up a disproportionate share of the people who were angry about it,' she told me, before offering up another gem: 'Regardless of the numbers, black women occupied a special role in this public spectacle, as the "chosen home" community for Dolezal. They were in the unique and unusually powerful position to be gatekeepers, to embrace or reject her. So it's not surprising that some of them would treat her as an interloper, a usurper.'

It was one of the motivations of outrage that I had yet to consider; perhaps outrage was simply the opportunity for the powerless to be powerful for a day. An emancipation of sorts. Black women, often placed on the bottom rung of the social ladder, were in a rare position of supremacy and were milking every drip of their temporary dominion in the Dolezal saga. As the gatekeepers of black womanhood, the very thing Rachel Dolezal was trying to access, we could grant or deny entry to our social circle and, according to Rachel, we chose the latter.

Dr Morning was adamant that judging people's identities in moral terms was an ineffective way to gain social insights, so venting our frustrations about how someone else chose to identify actually served no progressive purpose whatsoever. I wondered then if our outrage had an entirely different motivation, one that had little to do with Rachel herself.

Wasn't it feasible that online mobs could indeed be formed, not out of genuine outrage, but out of a subconscious need for control? I began to consider whether many of these outrage stampedes were mutual networks of oppressed people, taking offence at things that represented the social structures holding them down; faking our outrage in an attempt to regain some semblance of authority, however temporary. Were we even aware that our outrage could be spurred on by this desire? When it came to Rachel Dolezal were we pretending to be outraged, just like she was pretending to be black?

Outrage is triggered by any behaviour that violates our moral codes and it is this shared value system that forms the ties that build a tribe. This might mean plussize communities speaking out against body shaming, women speaking out against gender inequality and Muslims speaking out against Islamophobia. Or it could just as easily mean cisgender women denying the rights of transgender women, fascists opposing the free movement of immigrants or the Swifties feuding with the BeyHive. In academic terms this is known as social identity theory and refers to the self-categorising that creates the boundaries of 'them' and 'us'.

So are we using outrage to empower our comrades and ourselves? Echoing their responses in order to strengthen our allegiances? Are we just hyping each other up with declarations of rage that ricochet around the echo chamber through likes and retweets while legitimising the behaviour of the mob?

Much of this tribal outrage seems to be a way of proving that we back our communities. By being collectively agitated, we realign ourselves with our social kinfolk, fighting every perceived threat to these unions in order to prove how radical we are willing to be on behalf of the team.

But in matters of outrage these teams can quickly become mobs.

And it's the mob that seems to be stifling the power of outrage.

It was then that I realised Rachel Dolezal may have been right. Maybe the lion's share of the outrage she experienced *had* been at the hands of black women. But perhaps this was less about Rachel and more about the mob. The target of the outrage was inconsequential; it was the swarm behind it that told the story.

Black women stood to gain the most from the communal takedown of Rachel Dolezal. It offered power to a group that the world would have you believe were powerless. It galvanised the tribe and reaffirmed the sisterhoods within it. It gave a platform to the voices she had attempted to replace and in doing so provided a vehicle for conversations that might have otherwise gone unheard.

But by sitting in our bubbles, regurgitating each other's hot takes and looking inwardly for the approval of our tribe, we were losing the communal fighting spirit that had once got things done. Where movement en masse once provided progress through resistance, it seemed to have become a means of resisting progress. No longer were we pushing towards a common cause by pooling our outrage, instead we had become completely fragmented and aimlessly combative.

Rather than using our strength in numbers to reshape attitudes, we were using it to drag and cancel them. It was as though social media, the very thing that was intended to connect us, had in fact created an infrastructure that was leaving us more divided than ever.

3

OUTRAGE-MONGERS

Fine. I'll hold my hands up again... I too have misspent my outrage. And it was an absolute farce.

Picture the scene. It's 2014. Barack Obama is President of the United States, Kim Kardashian's greasy bum is on the cover of *PAPER* magazine and Piers Morgan has just written a column for the *Daily Mail* in which he attempts to explain to African Americans exactly where they are going wrong in their attempts to eradicate use of 'the N word'. (Because of course a privately schooled Sussex boy is the obvious choice for expert commentary on critical race realism and the history of black consciousness.)

'The reason it is so ingrained in pop culture,' he wrote, 'is that many blacks, especially young blacks reared to the soundtrack of N-word splattered rap music, use it in an ironic way.'

I was outraged. So outraged, in fact, that I wrote an open letter to the little bundle of bigotry and posted it on Twitter.

It began:

Dear Piers, your 'n-word' article was very valid but reeked of superiority. We do not need you to be our judge, jury or hero. Your argument was delivered as though it was some sort of self-serving epiphany. As if you had finally found the answer to a problem that has plagued our community for years. But in reality, you do not have the authority, nor the social experience, to comment on the roots of an issue which far exceeds your realm of middle-class comprehension...

The letter was viewed over 100,000 times and eventually Piers himself reposted it, adding a brief note: 'Dear Dotty, thanks for the patronising lecture...'

I'll be completely honest here: my heroic moment of vigilante outrage was thrilling (albeit temporarily). My Twitter mentions were on fire. I bagged myself scores of new followers and received a flurry of ecstatic texts from friends saying: 'OMG Piers just replied to you!' I had spoken up on behalf of my tribe and the reputational rewards were flooding in. I felt like Moses. But as the retweets slowed down (and I suffered the crippling realisation that my near-perfect letter to Piers had in fact included a sodding typo), I began to see the error of my ways. Like some sort of social media rookie, I had played directly into his grubby hands. I had been so quick to react that I hadn't even seen his article for what it was: clickbait.

You see, back in 2014, the former *Daily Mirror* editor was still reeling from the cancellation of his CNN ratings-killer *Piers Morgan Tonight*. 'It's been a painful period and lately we have taken a bath in the ratings,' Morgan told the *New York Times* when it was revealed that the cable network would be pulling the plug. 'I am a British guy debating American cultural issues, including guns, which has been very polarising, and there is no doubt that there are many in the audience who are tired of me banging on about it,' he added.

Six months after the show was axed, Piers was on the brink of a comeback, with the *Mail Online* announcing him as their new US editor-at-large. 'He has vast experience as an editor and presenter and certainly knows how to generate conversation and create debate so we're delighted that he will be joining us,' said Martin Clarke, the website's publisher and editor-in-chief.

This, we would soon find out, was an understatement.

What better way to reassert some journalistic pulling power in your new job than to write an article on a contentious subject that was guaranteed to get a reaction? And so we were duly served his cunningly titled editorial debut: IF BLACK AMERICANS WANT THE N-WORD TO DIE, THEY WILL HAVE TO KILL IT THEMSELVES.

In an instant, Piers Morgan was being talked about everywhere from BBC News to Al Jazeera, notching up a considerable amount of free advertising space for Brand Morgan. His incendiary rhetoric had gone viral, and with every disgruntled reader who had publicly condemned his column came another handful of clicks.

'Is it what I wrote that offended, #BlackTwitter – or the skin colour of the man who wrote it? #Nword,' Piers taunted on his Twitter page, stoking the coals of outrage shortly after the column went live.

'You are further evidencing your deep ignorance. Black people have been debating this among themselves long before you,' responded the journalist and author Ta-Nehisi Coates.

'If you don't understand white privilege, you must check out @piersmorgan's article today,' posted the civil rights activist DeRay Mckesson, joining the Twitter conversation.

Fuelled by outrage and propelled into action, we unwittingly spread his column worldwide.

Provocation quickly became Piers Morgan's online business model and three years later he regurgitated his article – this time responding to a viral video of some white female college students who were shown rapping the offensive word at a sorority party – with the rejigged *Daily Mail* headline: DON'T GET ANGRY ABOUT A BUNCH OF WHITE GIRLS SINGING N***AS, BLAME KANYE AND THE RAP INDUSTRY FOR PUTTING IT IN THEIR SONGS IN THE FIRST PLACE. 'I will inevitably provoke outrage from certain quarters, but that outrage is also an important and relevant factor for the purposes of this column,' he wrote.

And of course, outrage followed once more. He had found a winning formula – and I had lost big time.

Piers was my outrage epiphany. A sobering realisation that I'd been royally played like a well-tuned guitar at an Ed Sheeran gig. My outrage was breathing life into a narrative I had intended to kill. It was then that I realised I was a pawn in a bigger societal game. One that pitted the buyers of rage against the purveyors. And the rage-mongers were likely to win.

Unsurprisingly, orchestrated blowback, designed to provoke a response, is a tried and tested model for interaction in the digital age. In 2014, researchers at Beihang University in China found that rage is the sentiment that travels fastest online and that negative headlines collect

30 per cent more views than positive ones, with people more likely to click through to articles that include negative superlatives like 'worst'. Our curiosity, they found, is triggered more by anger than by any other human emotion and it is these stories that we are most likely to share... furiously.

There is an unwritten rule in journalism that predates the Internet: 'If it bleeds it leads' – a long-standing mantra that has taught newsrooms to prioritise stories that provoke fear or unrest. LONDON'S MURDER EPIDEMIC WORSE THAN NEW YORK'S; ECONOMY IN RUIN: WORST ON RECORD. These are the headlines we live for. Why report that TWO THIRDS OF BRITS SLEEP PEACEFULLY IN THEIR BEDS when you could spin it to read ONE IN THREE BRITS PLAGUED BY INCURABLE INSOMNIA? It is no wonder then that articles based on harm and disorder sit at the top of the news story hierarchy.

Isn't it likely then, that ambitious and enterprising media personalities are putting this same algorithm for engagement to good use, trading controversy for fame and building their own brand of notoriety by feeding our predisposed negativity bias? Are we even aware of how often we are falling for their deliberate provocation?

And maybe it isn't just the self-styled villains who stand to profit from our discontent. After all, the carefully curated careers of your liberal faves are also reliant on the booming trend of outrage. Their think pieces, panel appearances and self-help books are hinged on social unrest. They need us to view everything as racist, sexist, non-inclusive cultural appropriation, otherwise who will commission their 2,000-word hot takes and invite them to give TED Talks?

I was convinced that outrage-mongers were the new architects of unrest. And I was desperate to speak to one of them.

The usual suspects came to mind... Kelvin MacKenzie, a seasoned outrage-monger with over thirty-five years' experience in the bigotry business. The former editor of the *Sun* newspaper had been at the helm from 1981 to 1994 and oversaw such joyous headlines as AIDS IS THE WRATH OF GOD in 1985. There was also Tomi Lahren, the resident mischief-maker on Fox News, who shockingly tweeted 'meet the new KKK, they call themselves #BlackLivesMatter'. Of course my old adversary Piers Morgan was another option. I even considered Katie Hopkins, a divisive figure on the British media circuit, who once compared refugees to cockroaches.

I blasted a few email enquiries to my motley crew of media rebels and intermittently refreshed my inbox in the hope that one of them would respond.

From: Katie Hopkins
Date: Monday, 16 April 2018 at 04:41
To: Ashley Charles
Subject: Hopkins

Hey Ashley
Hopkins here. Happy to help.
Can natter on my phone if you want to give me a call. 07*** *** ***.

K
@KTHopkins
Telling it like it is

And just like that, I had Katie Hopkins's mobile number. But before we get into that, some context.

Katie Hopkins is a professional bitch; a title-holder in ethical limbo who somehow manages to stoop lower even when you think the bar is already on the floor. Her ascent to notoriety was an unlikely one, having first found relative fame as the mouthy cow from series three of *The Apprentice*, and since then her wanton malevolence has granted her the title of 'celebrity'.

Katie Hopkins's media CV reads like a criminal record. She has been hired, fired, sued and detained for her inflammatory views and was even immortalised in the provocatively titled musical *The Assassination of Katie Hopkins*, a performance about public debate written by the playwright and lyricist Chris Bush.

In 2015, a United Nations human rights commissioner Zeid Ra'ad Al Hussein spoke out in a statement against one of Katie Hopkins's columns for the *Sun* in which she had courted controversy by describing immigrants as cockroaches. 'History has shown us time and again the dangers of demonising foreigners and minorities,' he said, 'and it is extraordinary and deeply shameful to see these types of tactics being used in a variety of countries, simply because racism and xenophobia are so easy to arouse in order to win votes or sell newspapers.'

By 2016, Katie had left the *Sun* and was writing for its competitors at the *Mail Online*, who were soon forced to pay out £150,000 in damages after a court ruled that she had used her new column to falsely accuse a Muslim family of extremism. In 2017, she was sacked from her controversial radio show on LBC after using Nazi hate speech to comment on terrorism during another of her anti-Muslim tirades on Twitter. In the contentious tweet she called for a 'final solution' against Islamic extremism, echoing the term for genocide used by the Third Reich during the Holocaust. 'Having read her latest article, it's hard to think of anything left for Katie Hopkins to do now, other than to just kill some people,' tweeted British actor Matt Lucas after one of her outrageous rants.

Within a few years, she had reached fifth gear, and during a keynote speech at the David Horowitz Freedom Center's 'Restoration Weekend 2017' in Florida ('an activist-minded battle tank' that seeks to 'identify America's enemies and fight the Left'), Hopkins, by now a seasoned provocateur, said: 'I am a straight, white, conservative female with one husband and three children under thirteen, and where I come from, back in Blighty, that virtually makes me an endangered species. I'm on the extinctions list, the list of animals that are due for extinction. I'm up there with the black rhino, and he has an advantage because he's black. Black lives matter, people.'

Katie uses hate speech to arouse the easily outraged. She is an experienced agitator who knows exactly how to elicit the public's widespread fury, and we, in turn, propagate her bullish brand of bigotry by giving it the attention it seeks. Anyone who has ever engaged with Katie Hopkins, even if it was to launch all manner of expletives at her, is a dogsbody in her outrage racket – helping to keep the lights on in her suburban cave.

But taking the bait is at times impossible to resist. 'Torn between wanting to continue ignoring Katie Hopkins, and finding out where she lives and running her over with a tank,' Caitlin Moran once tweeted. Ditto.

We thrive on the depravity of characters like Katie Hopkins because they satisfy our need to engage in moral combat by providing us with a villain against which our own ethics can be measured. But are deliberate wrong'uns like Hopkins just red herrings in our pursuit of moral progression? Although we believe that by taking them on we are playing a role in some sort of restorative justice, are we in fact engaging in misplaced outrage?

I wondered whether Katie Hopkins even believed the extremist dross she spouted, or if it was all the invention of a well-crafted character that she plays. Could her constant derision of race, religion and class simply be an audacious performance? Was this simply provocation for profit?

I hovered anxiously over the dial button for an inordinate amount of time, wondering how often Katie Hopkins changed phone numbers, given how easily she had sent hers to me, a complete stranger. Perhaps she had a drawer full of burner phones and this was just the SIM card she used on Mondays. I should hurry up and call. I put it off for another hour, drafted some conversational bullet points, then opted for a text instead.

We went back and forth with time and date suggestions, attempting to schedule an interview between her media engagements and medical appointments (she was having her arm socket rebuilt after an epilepsy-related injury). She was surprisingly accommodating and even suggested that we meet up in person for coffee in the city. Fuck that,

I thought to myself. Being seen at a table for two with the most hated woman in Britain? I bloody think not. So I made my excuses (some nonsense about travelling abroad) and we arranged to speak on the phone instead.

After a false start owing to a patchy phone signal, she gave me her landline number and it dawned on me that I now had more means of contacting Katie Hopkins than I did for my actual friends.

It was approaching 7.30 p.m. on a Monday evening, and a week had passed since her first email, when I finally dialled her number.

'Hello, Katie speaking!' She answered brightly after two rings. Her tone was disarmingly chipper. If I hadn't known who was on the other end of the phone I would have pictured one of those lively spin-class mums that are hopped-up on Americanos at 7 a.m., jogging their kids to school in Lululemon activewear.

'Thank you so much for taking the time out to speak to me!' I say, attempting to match her sprightly mood and get our chat started on a good footing, and after a few high-pitched pleasantries we dive right in.

I ask her whether she considers herself a villain.

'I think the villainy idea is a little simplistic, actually,' she says. 'I think it's what people do to rationalise the things I say. I think that in order to make it OK that there's people like me who think the things I think, it's much easier for people and their tiny minds to imagine that I'm a monster or a villain. And that makes them think, *Oh, she's a monster and a villain and therefore she's talking nonsense and I can disregard it totally*.'

I wonder whether the tone I had at first mistaken as chipper was in fact manic self-assurance. I begin to picture her with that deranged smile she wears on her face when she's feeling particularly smug. A look I knew well.

'I guess it's strange or hard for people when they meet me in person, or get to know me, or have interactions with me on a normal basis; they're really shocked,' she continues. 'Mostly people say how small I am, because monsters are supposed to be big, I think. And other people are shocked because I'm *super super super* normal, pretty fine to work with and not at all scary, and that becomes *super* confusing for them because they much preferred it when it was a villain saying the things I say than just a regular mum of three who's quite small.' She rambles excessively, veering off-topic in an instant. She seems enamoured with the sound of her own voice.

I feel as though I've landed myself front-row tickets to the Katie Hopkins panto and ask her whether the public version of herself is an exaggerated version of who she really is.

'I think they're pretty consistent,' she says. 'I mean, we see really crap villains come and go. There was this woman, I can't even remember her name, which is indicative. She had massive boobs and she had them done on the NHS. Then she was on *This Morning* and she was talking about how the NHS boobs had helped her in her career as a glamour model and we're all supposed to be outraged because that's the taxpayers' money! And that's really simplistic as a model for debate. It's very clickbaity and it's pathetic villainy that doesn't have any depth to it.'

I can't see quite where she's going with this but, shifting the phone to my other ear, I let her go on. Eventually she arrives at her point. She tells me that her own longevity in the public eye is proof of the authenticity behind her brand. 'For me to have been around for as long as I have, and bugger me, I feel like I've been around a long time now, there has to be something in what you're saying and I think you have to really believe it or you'd be contradicting yourself all over the place,' she says.

'I think what's hard for people who disagree with me, which I completely accept, is that I really believe the stuff I say,' she continues. 'I really believe the stuff I say about migrants, or people who I consider less useful than myself, or people who I consider lazy. I've got no problem with that.'

I sit up in my chair, wondering how exhausting it would be to remain convincingly in character for more than a decade. If Katie Hopkins' public persona is indeed an act, it is certainly one that she has had ample opportunity to rehearse in the years since she first landed on our TV screens in 2006. So I follow intently, listening out for a tell in her voice and noticing that her tone has calmed significantly. 'I am this way and I always have been,' she insists confidently.

I wondered which of her outrageous comments Katie Hopkins attributed to the start of her prickly relationship with the public, so I asked what she thought she had done to first get people's backs up.

'The name thing was the thing that kind of started that off, with me saying, "Look, I'd never call my kid Tyler,"' she recalls, referring to *that* baby name fiasco of 2013. A TV moment that is hard to forget. It was July 2013 and Katie had been invited onto ITV's daily feature programme *This Morning* to discuss popular baby names. A car crash ensued. In fact, 'car crash' is far too tame for Katie. This was a seven-car pile-up with no survivors.

She expressed her disdain for 'the Tylers, the Charmaines, the Chantelles, the Chardonnays', suggesting that a name is a 'shortcut' and an 'efficient way to work out what [social] class that child comes from'. She went as far as saying that she would prevent her own children from socialising with other kids according to this name-based prejudice. According to Katie, children without 'intelligent names' are financially poor, disruptive in class and less likely to do their homework. She was plucking sociological theories out of her arse as we sat at home watching with our mouths agape. And as we granted her that coveted media trophy – attention – Katie Hopkins hit the jackpot. She had found her niche and it was outrage.

She continued her tirade online, hauling the volatile narrative for another twenty-four hours. Tyronnes were thugs and Jaydens were benefit cheats. 'Tyronne … not too many steps to tyranny is it? One small step for man, one giant leap for thug kind,' she tweeted. She was a runaway train hurtling her way to notoriety. In the months that followed she disparaged fat people, full-time mums, working women, unemployed women, redheads, Ramadan. Even Glaswegians weren't safe from her Twitter fingers. 'Sending us Ebola bombs in the form of sweaty Glaswegians just isn't cricket. Scottish NHS sucks,' she wrote on her Twitter page after a man from Glasgow contracted the Ebola virus.

'But I didn't hide from that,' she continues on the phone. 'I'm not a villain who throws a hand grenade and then runs away. I turned up to do the school run the next day, to face up to my stuff—'

'What was that like?' I interrupt.

'I mean, it was no different to normal, really. School-gate mums aren't really fans of working mums. They never are,' she says in a way that suggests she is lining up one of her scathing punchlines. 'They turn up in their pyjamas and their Uggs and so any mother who bothered to maybe shower or wear a suit they can't really comprehend or talk to. And that's *super* fine by me, actually.'

But I wonder if she really is as unbothered as she behaves. 'Do you ever fear for your life, based on how many people feel about you?' I ask.

'Errrrrm.' She pauses. Perhaps she is at least slightly flappable. 'No. Not at all,' she says. 'Clearly there has been a *real risk to life*. The police consider it a risk to life. Two jihadis were put down last year. They're now inside for plotting to behead me.'

Yes. Katie Hopkins was the target of a foiled assassination plot in 2015 when the aspiring jihadi Madihah Taheer, who was later convicted of conspiring to commit acts of terrorism with her boyfriend, colluded in plans to kill a list of targets that included Hopkins. Yet Katie talks about the incident as if someone was simply caught stealing her garden gnomes. 'I don't fear for myself at all,' she continues. 'I feel weirdly invincible and I think that's why I don't have fear. I don't feel fear now at all, not in any situation, not amongst a mob at Speakers' Corner or anywhere else, actually. No one really frightens me,' she says. 'I do know there are people out to kill me and I accept that... If you say stuff people don't like, one way they'll look to silence you is to end you. Our state does it as well to people who they put inside and allow the Muslim prison population to kill.'

Worried that she might be leading me down a bizarre cul-de-sac of conspiracy theories, I try and redirect the conversation back to her would-be assailant, Madihah Taheer. I ask whether the beheading fantasy made her rethink her goading of Islam.

'I love the way the *Guardian* and others used the word "fantasy" about that as well,' she says in a bullish voice that suggested she didn't love it at all. 'I'm sure if it was Stella Creasy or Owen Jones or Diane Abbott it wouldn't be a fantasy. It would be an "outrageous attack" or a "racist attack". But with me, it's a "fantasy of beheading". I love the way the Left do that … I may have become a little averse to Islam after those practising the religion wanted to chop my head off,' she went on. 'I don't think that's altogether surprising, but it doesn't make me frightened of them. In fact, if I met them face to face I'm pretty sure I'd do better than them, either in an argument or a physical fight. So no, I don't feel afraid and I certainly wouldn't change the way I am.'

'So you think you'd win in a fist fight with some jihadis?' I ask.

She laughs awkwardly, as though she hadn't meant for the conversation to take this absolutely bizarre turn. Which makes two of us. 'I don't think about that, but there's been Charlotte Church, who wanted to do a boxing match, and then I said yes and then she backed out. Then, what's that ridiculous woman with the high-pitched voice that only dogs can hear? Ellie Goulding. She wanted to fist fight me.

I think it's people with lower intelligence who seek to use their fists first, and Charlotte Church and Ellie Goulding are probably very good examples of that.'

I caught myself smirking silently and willed myself not to be amused by a woman whose views were so clearly offensive. But I found it hard to believe that this wasn't all just an elaborate comedy act. 'People do say I should do stand-up,' she tells me proudly.

In between outrageous remarks, Katie oddly repositioned herself as completely normal. 'If you could see me now,' she says. 'I'm in my pyjamas. My kids are upstairs. I'm this little me. And so it's bonkers and laughable and beyond ridiculous that I could possibly be the biggest threat to race relations in the twentieth century.'

Although she plays down her toxic rhetoric as 'bonkers' and 'laughable', Katie Hopkins is in fact a severe moral offender. She was questioned by the Metropolitan Police Homicide and Major Crime Command over her comments on migrants and even landed herself in custody for spreading racial hatred in South Africa.

'I don't think I'll ever be the issue,' she claims defiantly. But what she downplays in narrow-mindedness she certainly makes up for in self-confidence.

'I just have a way, don't I? I have a way of speaking, I have a way with my voice, I have a way with words. That's my craft,' she says, when I ask whether her style of speech is deliberately provocative. 'My tool is words and my craft is being able to craft words,' she continues. 'The average person in the street is just a bit stupid. That doesn't make me the problem — they should have worked harder at school. I think you're inferring that I'm the one who's exaggerating. I'd just say that most people have a low level of language ability.' I roll my eyes so far back I almost lose a contact lens.

We start to talk about privilege and minorities, with Katie lapping up the opportunity to force-feed me her insolent one-liners. Her ignorant remarks about Ramadan make me physically recoil. But was it all just an exercise in image preservation? Was she simply saying things that fit with her outrageous facade?

'It almost seems like there is a degree of brand management that you have to do for Brand Katie, which means keeping the wilder statements out there, continuing to kind of sell that angle of outrage,' I suggest.

'I totally appreciate what you're saying and in no way am I saying you're wrong, but I think that's slightly outdated,' she says. 'Now I'm really, *really* committed to getting out and doing stories on the ground. So, Sweden, crossing from Libya to Sicily, getting to South Africa for three weeks. I'm on my way to Syria, hopefully very soon,' she adds, sounding like she's appointed herself Minister of Foreign Affairs.

'So this Katie Hopkins that I'm talking to now, who seems to have journalistic integrity, does she regret anything that the slightly more controversial Katie Hopkins has said, such as *immigrants are cockroaches*?' I ask.

'No. Because I think that's all your path, isn't it. I think if you back up and you bring up your path, then if you were trying to retrace it or let someone follow it and see your mistakes, I think you need to leave those in. Like the potholes in your past. I think those are really important,' she says, her voice dropping wistfully. 'I miss certain things. I miss my radio show. And not for the bloody radio show. I couldn't care less. But I really miss speaking to people in their kitchen on a Sunday at ten. So I regret that. I regret the fallout of my mighty mouth.' I relax in my seat for the first time during our call, feeling as though I might actually be talking to the real Katie Hopkins.

'There's a lot of noise out there,' she adds with another flicker of sincerity. 'So we have to think a bit more about what noise we actually contribute.'

I was now inwardly questioning whether the Katie Hopkins we knew was a lie that had been based on a loose truth. Like when you have a tickly cough but exaggerate it into full-blown bronchitis to get the day off work. It's not entirely false; it's just strategically overstated – an opportunistic embellishment that fits your agenda.

Katie Hopkins is outrageous, but not as much as she would have you believe. Her modus operandi is simply to keep you engaged by any sleaze necessary. She is careful not to fall out of character, but unwittingly shows signs of normality that at times borders on, dare I say it... congeniality. I wondered whether I was speaking to a woman in transition, a self-made villain who perhaps sensed the jig was almost up.

'Do you think your rhetoric has an expiration date?' I ask.

'I guess there's an evolution there and I think I'm still moving forwards; at least I hope I am, and I'm not bored of myself yet. Maybe that's the point – when I'm bored of myself, I will either top myself or give up.'

Katie's obsession with controversy seemed to be part business plan, part coping mechanism. She's had her fair share of private struggles after all, including life-threatening epilepsy (of which she claims she has now been cured), an unfaithful first husband who abandoned her with two children, and a totally avoidable collision with insolvency (less than six months after we spoke, Katie was forced to sell her five-bedroom house after losing a libel case). I wouldn't be surprised if she'd considered walking out into a busy intersection and ending it all. Of course, most people are able to overcome their personal troubles without becoming vile stains on the fabric of humanity in the process, but Katie, it seems, has very little morale worth losing.

'Would you rather be hated than ignored?' I quizzed her.

'No, I don't think I'd rather be hated, I think I accept absolutely being hated for my views and I accept that it extends beyond views for people. A lot of people are like "if I ever saw her I'd smack her in the face" ... But I accept that completely. If you go out there and you say your stuff or you put yourself out there, expect that. Never complain about that. That's part of the deal. But would I be happy being ignored? As long as I was doing my thing well, I'm fine with being ignored. That would be fine with me.'

Somehow I'm not convinced.

In 2015, appearing on *Celebrity Big Brother*, Katie Hopkins said: 'I don't give offence; you choose to take it and you need to make better decisions.' And it would have been very straightforward for us to silence Katie Hopkins a long time ago, simply by starving her of attention.

You see, the people who are most outraged by her are the same people who propelled her to stardom. Maybe you have been tricked into thinking that *your* interactions with her are different. Perhaps you're convinced that taking her on makes you in some way morally valiant. I was convinced of the same thing when I decided to lock horns with Piers Morgan. But campaigning to have her removed from platforms or signing a petition to swap her for 50,000 refugees (yes, this was a real petition and yes, 61,407 people signed it), simply adds cogs to her PR wheel.

'So people who are offended by you, do you think they're maybe spending their outrage in the wrong place? Do you think their outrage would be better spent on something else?' I ask.

'Yeah, I think so,' she says. 'I get that they're cross, but then I see that maybe linguistically or physically or otherwise they haven't found a way to expend their excess energy and so they're just channelling it at me. And my thing would always be to challenge it well and that definitely doesn't mean drawing up a petition. If I see another petition I will launch my terrible PC out of my window. It's definitely not about a march, or a walk in a silly hat with a banner or otherwise. I think it's the same challenge that I put to myself: how do you effect change?'

I remind her about one of her recent sarky tweets that read, 'I identify as a black lesbian on Thursdays after 2pm. Please respect my decision and call me Shyanne at this time.' I explain to her that although her intention may have been to antagonise black gay women like myself, it actually had the opposite effect. I hadn't reacted at all. 'I wonder, do you think people are gonna reach that point of indifference, where you've said it all and now it's water off a duck's back?' I ask.

'Yeah, of course!' she enthuses, as if she's already reserved her spot in line at the Job Centre. 'I'm sure thousands, if not hundreds of thousands, already have. I'm sure hundreds of thousands are so bored of me they've probably got me on mute, or have unfollowed or never want to see me ever again. And I get that. We all have cycles in life. The black lesbian thing... I was doing kind of a gag about the whole gender thing because it does do my nut in slightly. But yes, I think people will tire of me, have tired of me. You know, I think that's a great thing. That's kind of my message also: you've got your own little remote control on life and you can press "off".'

And for the first time I agree wholeheartedly with the wicked witch of Exeter. It is time to change the channel.

'I don't see myself as the baddie in this,' she says. 'I know we started off with villainy, but I think it might actually turn out that I'm the secret fairy godmother... Maybe in a really crap costume.'

As our interview began to come to its end I bluntly remark: 'I thought I'd come out of this conversation thinking "she's an evil genius" or "she's a piece of shit". And I'm leaning towards evil genius.'

'Ahh well, that's OK,' she says. 'A piece of shit would have been all right too, actually.'

4

SHITSTORMS AND SNOWFLAKES

With Katie's words ringing in my ear, I thought back to Rachel Dolezal and what she had said about outrage being a tool. That it could be used for good and it could be used for evil. So are we just using it wrong?

Imagine if we took the efforts we were investing so freely in the takedown of people and focused them into the destabilisation of power structures. Would we not be putting our outrage to better use if, instead of using it to 'cancel' Rachel Dolezal, we used it to disrupt the systems that truly proliferate black oppression? Were we mad at Katie Hopkins or at the broader, institutionalised bigotry to which she subscribes? Was Piers Morgan really the problem or was it the media gatekeepers who enable and empower his deeply flawed (and infuriatingly smug) rhetoric?

And then I remembered something else Rachel had said, an idea my memory now latched on to, playing on a constant loop. 'When my story got thrown into the media, everybody was like: *She didn't ask for permission; she just took this,*' Rachel had said, describing the accusations of cultural appropriation that had been levelled at her for, among other things, braiding her hair. 'So [there are] all these assumptions about cultural appropriation and I feel like in a sense what's actually being appropriated is activism.'

I wasn't sure I had given this the attention it deserved at the time, perhaps letting my cynicism about the messenger distract from the message. But now it seemed an inspired notion.

'The problem with outrage in its modern guise is that posts and retweets have replaced pickets and sit-ins,' she had said, with the loaded stare and overzealous nod of a would-be cult leader in the pulpit. 'The key to effective action, effective advocacy, effective activism, is to organise and channel outrage in a way that fulfils a purpose and accomplishes a goal. Right now, there's just a whole big quagmire of stuff online.'

'It's like activism appropriation,' she repeated. 'Because people are hijacking the movement [with] cheap sound bites, and the attention span doesn't even last long enough to actually get anything done.'

Maybe that was it. Activism has been appropriated.

By now I was becoming a bit of an activism purist, which is rich coming from me, someone with little to no protest experience, but still, I couldn't help but daydream about outrage in its prime. One dreary Tuesday morning, around about the time I started writing this part of the book, I was sat in a taxi on my way to do a radio show at the arse-crack of dawn, when I found myself thinking back to an old-school group of activists my mum had told me about during another one of her extra-curricular dinner-table lessons in the nineties. (The school syllabus was trying to convince us that Christopher Columbus was a hero, so she felt obliged to give us some black-history balance.) They were the Greensboro Four, a defiant quartet of black students from a North Carolina college who sat at the whites only lunch counter of retail powerhouse F. W. Woolworth's to peacefully protest the Jim Crow laws of America's segregated South.

Having been denied service at the counter, the four remained stubbornly seated until the store closed, and they returned the following day with dozens more students. Scores more from neighbouring colleges returned on the third day and by the fourth the sit-in had swelled to include hundreds of young protestors who were, at this point, completely crippling the store. In the weeks that followed, state-wide sit-ins were staged across more than fifty cities in America. Until finally, in the summer of 1960, after six months of protest, Woolworth's desegregated their lunch counter, along with many other newly integrated diners across the Southern states.

My memory of the Greensboro Four had begun to fade slightly over the years though, so after wrapping up *The Breakfast Show* I fired up my laptop (an out-of-warranty aluminium slab that I bought in 2012 but am too cheap to replace) and began to fill in the gaps of what had become a blurry history lesson. It was then that I came across an interview between Joseph McNeil, one of the four, and a historian by the name of Eugene Pfaff, transcribed from a collection of recordings at the Greensboro Public Library in 1979.

Eugene Pfaff asked:

'What do you think it was that resulted in the desegregation of the lunch counters, the theatres, the cafeterias, that sort of thing? Was it the economic boycotting pressure brought by the black community or some other factor?'

McNeil's response is an unintentional masterclass in effective outrage:

There's certainly no denying that the economics, I think, had an effect. I don't recall the figures from Woolworth's now, but I do think it did have an impact. The other pressures, the continuing pressure, for example, [that] we could fill the jails. We could literally break the city government by filling the jails, if it came to that point, if they [wanted] to arrest us, we could fill the jails and stay there for six months. It became such a terrible problem for the city government to try to manage that, not to mention the ill-press and world opinion, aside from the economics of the matter. That was the type of pressure that eventually brought about a change... It's extremely brilliant, in the sense that we called into effect and coordinated such a massive group of things and people. For a group of seventeen, eighteen, nineteen-year-olds – we coordinated press releases, national speaking engagements, demonstrations on a day-to-day basis, legal efforts; we went around to churches and made speeches trying to make the movement grow and solicit aid and help for those who needed contributions, we helped raise money for the NAACP. All of that was a heck of a lot for a group of seventeen, eighteen and nineteen-year-olds to coordinate. Not just from a coordination point of view, but from the phys-ical presence aspects – showing up each day, manning the picket line with the right type of people.

I sat there mouth agape. My eighteen-year-old brother couldn't coordinate a prayer circle in a Baptist church.

Before the Internet age, activism was truly active. In 1950s Montgomery, Alabama, an entire generation of freedom fighters voted with their feet and boycotted the city's segregated buses for 381 days. African Americans, who accounted for 75 per cent of the city's bus riders, refused to step on board a single bus and in doing so, forced the federal and Supreme courts to integrate public transport.

Not even that long ago, in 1995, an ancient time before smartphones and WiFi hotspots, Louis Farrakhan had gathered hundreds of thousands of African American men in what is remembered in history as 'The Million Man March'. The demonstration did not carry a singular objective. It was not a political protest, nor was it particularly intended as a show of outrage. It was, in fact, an introspective call to action – an ambitious show of like-mindedness intended to instil a sense of unity and accountability among black men in America. It was widely reported that over 1.5 million African American men registered to vote in the months that followed. Yes, a million men (or thereabouts) could congregate without Facebook checkpoints or Insta-stories and they could gather not just for protest but for progress.

Fast-forward to October 2017, when #WomenBoycott Twitter was trending worldwide. A uniquely absurd attempt at activism in the digital age, the plan was for a moderately ambitious social media blackout that would protest Twitter's alleged silencing of Harvey Weinstein accuser Rose McGowan. So women began pledging their absence, promising to log out of their Twitter accounts for twenty-four hours in a show of solidarity. Because that'll teach those Twitter execs not to mess with us gals. One measly day of inactivity.

I had come across the hashtag a day earlier when my beloved Chrissy Teigen posted: 'Tomorrow. And maybe even forever. #WomenBoycottTwitter.'

Panicking that my favourite tweeter might forsake me in the name of hashtag activism, I anxiously searched for related posts.

'Tomorrow (Friday the 13th) will be the first day in over 10 years that I won't tweet. Join me. #WomenBoycott Twitter,' posted @Alyssa_Milano.

'Ok ok Jesus, let me clear this up. #Women BoycottTwitter will not silence us, but @Twitter will make much less $$ b/c of fewer clicks. I'm in,' wrote comedian Kathy Griffin a few minutes later.

The hashtag was shared more than 190,000 times, but the conversations were happening on Twitter, which pretty much defeated the entire purpose of the boy-cott. It was business as usual for the social media plat-form without the slightest of dents in their operation, and after a day of meme withdrawals the digital activists were back online with their #MeToo posts and 'Is your boss a predator?' quizzes.

'Heads Up: I took a day off Twitter to protest #WomenBoycottTwitter, so expect TONS of ALL CAPS, OUTRAGE AND NAME CALLING,' posted writer and lawyer Amee Vanderpool (whose Twitter header reads 'Feminist') the following day.

All of those women taking a stand and not a single one throwing themselves under the king's horses? For shame! I mean, if you're going to boycott something then bloody boycott it. Deactivate your accounts, pull your advertising, chain yourselves to the company gates, shit in a box and mail it to the CEO.

But in our web-driven world, talking has replaced walking, giving way to a new breed of remonstration that looks to rid the world of every transgression one typo at a time. Activists are no longer the tireless protestors of America's Deep South, they are the idle-thumbed and semi-persecuted snowflakes of Twitter, setting the world bang-to-rights with their unlimited data plans. These days we see some moral or political deviance and hastily fire up one of our online apps to let the world know exactly how we feel about it. How on earth can we be expected to boycott transport when we've got yoga at 7 a.m. and a board meeting at 9 a.m. anyway?

Introducing clicktivism: it wants to be activism, but it just can't be arsed. It's the modern-day picket sign for the work-shy yet well intentioned who share their outrage through hashtags, online petitions and rambling captions about equal rights. Had a long day and couldn't get round to any real protesting? You need clicktivism! Feel like supporting a political campaign but also feel like taking an afternoon nap? How about clicktivism! Does your phone or tablet have WiFi connection and a hashtag button on the keypad?! Do you want to look like you're doing something while doing absolutely fuck-all? Did you fit the description of the virtue signallers in Chapter Two? I know just the thing… clicktivism!

In 2017, an online petition urging the UK government to intervene in the Libyan slave trade was signed by more than 265,000 Brits in three weeks. That's more than 12,000 people actively engaging in a cause every single day. Many of them, I imagine, spent the two minutes required to join a parliamentary petition before going about their usual routine. But how many of them bothered to attend the open gallery when Parliament eventually debated the topic in December of the same year? None. How many were even moderately aware of the response from the Foreign & Commonwealth Office, which stated: 'The Government shares the public's outrage and welcomes the Libyan government's commitment to investigate these reports and to ensure that those involved are brought to justice.'

I'll venture a guess that the 'commitment' of the outraged did not extend beyond the few clicks needed to share the petition and *appear* concerned.

Hashtag activism is visible almost every day on your social media platform of choice. So take your pick. There was #WalkOutMonday in September 2018, when people across America were wearing black and walking out of work to oppose rape culture. Then there was another one the following month when a bizarre 'emoji march' started happening on Twitter. It was just after 8 a.m. on 15 October 2018 when the digital demonstration got underway and it wasn't long before 2,000 Twitter users had joined. The objective was to push a 'Brexit People's Vote' through Parliament by 'marching'... and you didn't even have to put your shoes on for this one. 'RT our marching emojis to your local MP and show you support the #PeoplesVote March on 20 October. Let's get twitter marching…' read the tweet posted from the verified @ peoplesvote_uk account.

Honestly.

Perhaps the most significant turning point in the immobilisation of our outrage was the introduction of Facebook in 2006. By encouraging users to join groups and overtly align ourselves with like-minded allies, Mark Zuckerberg created a digital world in which it was easier than ever to pledge allegiance to a cause. It allowed us to frame our identities based on subscriptions to existing belief systems. You could be a feminist, a pro-life advocate, a protector of mythical reptiles – all with the click of a 'like' button. And without leaving the house.

There are now more than 18 million active Twitter users in Great Britain alone. The Chatty Patty platform, once intended for pictures of pets and real-time updates about the Super Bowl, has since become a place where facts sit alongside fake news, celebrities interact with trolls and anyone with an email address can be the national spokesperson of whateverthefucktheywant.

This shift in the gatekeeping of public opinion has meant that the route to outrage is easier than ever. Would I have been as outraged at Piers Morgan if it had required me to write a letter, find a postbox and then mail it to him? Would I heck! Who's got 70p for a postage stamp when tweeting is free anyway?

And so we find ourselves in the eye of the storm every time we open our apps. Ready to wage war over sugar

tax and MPs' expenses. Once upon a time outrage was
defined by resistance; now we are unable to resist it. We've
become so dedicated to the sport of outrage that they may
as well introduce it into the Summer Olympics. I for one
know four vegans who would nail the relay, and a *Guardian*
columnist who would be absolutely brilliant in the 400-
metre dragging.

In 2009, Anders Colding-Jørgensen, a behavioural psychologist and social media lecturer at the University of
Copenhagen who studies the way in which ideas spread
online, proved the extent of our recreational outrage by
getting people to join a Facebook group protesting plans
to tear down an iconic fountain in the Danish capital.

'No to Demolition of Stork Fountain' was the name of
the online group that opposed the city's plans to convert the
listed monument into an H&M store. Colding-Jørgensen
shared the group with his 150 Facebook friends and within
a few days, 300 people had joined the movement. By the
end of the week, there were 10,000 members, clicking,
sharing and 'protesting' online. When Colding-Jørgensen
decided to stop his experiment two weeks later, 27,000
people had pledged their support for the campaign.

But the crusade was entirely fictional. There were no
plans to demolish the monument. Twenty-seven thousand
people, sometimes joining at the rate of two a minute,
had jumped on board without even bothering to check
whether the cause was real or not. The group was 'in no
way useful for horizontal discussions', Colding-Jørgensen
said in an interview with the *Washington Post*. 'People just
went in and joined.'

Outrage is to the twenty-first century what pedal pushers were to the twentieth... irrationally on trend. It is virtually impossible to keep up with all the things we're supposed to be angry at. You take a day off Twitter for an offline detox and by the time you plug back in another miscellaneous celebrity has shit the bed. In fact I've come to realise that if a random rock star is suddenly trending they've either died or been caught with their proverbial dick out. Every time you open your social media app of choice, I can guarantee you are already late to at least one protest party. Try it. Head to Twitter now and take a look at the trending topics. I'm sure you'll find there are a few hundred people waxing lyrical about some atrocity you hadn't even heard of until this very second.

And working in radio, there is nothing worse than being late to the party. I mean, I get paid to know what the hell is going on and even I can't keep up with it all. Never has this been more apparent than when I made a shockingly belated arrival to the public dragging of TV chef Jamie Oliver in August 2018.

It was a slow news day when I finally noticed him trending on Twitter. I assumed that the menace to school dinners was either on some sugar-prohibition crusade or expecting baby number six with his foetus factory of a wife, a child whom he would inevitably give a name like Possum Hibiscus Disco. But it was something far, far worse. The son of a bitch was selling jerk rice. 'Punchy Jerk Rice' at £2.40 per microwaveable bag, to be precise. Twitter was up in arms. How very dare he. Jerk rice has never and will never be a thing. It exists nowhere other than in Jamie

Oliver's bizarre culinary imagination and the 'reduced to clear' section of Tesco.

Now, if you are less than au fait with the ninth wonder that is Jamaican food, let me be abundantly clear – jerk rice is as credible as pilau cheese or fried water in that it literally makes no sense (although Pizza Hut did once road-test a biryani pizza in its Sri Lankan branches back in 2013 – the Birizza). It is the ready-meal equivalent of when Jennifer Aniston rocked 'dreadlocks' to the 1999 Emmys – woefully misjudged. Jamie Oliver's little jalapeño-and-rice-pudding concoction was so laughable that I assumed we'd chuckle heartily at his audacious recipe for gentrified grains and get on with our days. Boy was I wrong. Because of course, outrage is way too stylish for us to pass up an opportunity like the cultural appropriation of cuisine.

And so began #Jerkgate: The Jamaican Inquisition. Anyone who had ever ordered a patty at their local Caribbean shop was suddenly a human rights activist specialising in the plagiarism of spicy goods. Labour MP Dawn Butler tweeted: '#jamieoliver @ jamieoliver #jerk I'm just wondering do you know what #Jamaican #jerk actually is? It's not just a word you put before stuff to sell products. Your jerk Rice is not ok. This appropriation from Jamaica needs to stop.' – @DawnButlerBrent

PR experts offered their views in a piece for trade magazine *PR Week*, endorsing the backlash against Jamie's 250g bag of lies. 'The Jamie Oliver story is one of straight-up misrepresentation,' said Warren Johnson from W Communications. 'Clearly the recipe has no jerk ingredients and therefore the product is totally misleading. Even before you get into any debates on cultural appropriation, this is a case of inaccurate information. He might as well say it has fairy dust in it too. In this case, you need to make an immediate apology and change the product name and information.'*

'There are a few observations and learnings on #jerkgate,' added PR guru Ruth Allchurch. 'Firstly, every consumer brand needs to understand that authenticity is king and food brands in particular should know that provenance is queen, so trying to 'fool' consumers is only likely to have a backlash.' And backlash was an understatement – the Outrage Express was only just leaving the station. *Good Morning Britain* waded in on the shitstorm with the headline JAMIE OLIVER RICE ROW as Jeremy Kyle chaired the live debate. Levi Roots, at the helm of a jerk-sauce empire (which, might I add, included the roll-out of a Reggae Reggae Pizza in 2011) called it a 'mistake' by Jamie Oliver, and ITV News even went on the streets to get scathing vox pops from actual black people. 'It's like shepherd's-pie mix,' said one hero after taking the taste test.

Now I'm not Jamie Oliver's biggest fan. He irks me for reasons I can't quite put my finger on. Like people who go through border control wearing a sombrero after a ten-day holiday in Cancun. I don't know exactly why it bothers me, it just does. But Jamie Oliver's totally tropical rice

---

* 'Over-heated debate or cultural appropriation? PR pros debate Jamie Oliver #Jerkgate', *PR Week*, 21 August 2018. https://www.prweek.com/article/1490859/over-heated-debate-cultural-appropriation-pr-pros-debate-jamie-oliver-jerkgate

certainly isn't the issue. Why? Because outrage should be reserved for things that actually impact our lives. How the fuck was Jamie Oliver's microwaveable farce ever going to impact me or anyone I knew? It wasn't affecting sales of genuine jerk products. My beloved Caribbean culture wasn't suffering any defamation as a result. Nobody was eating it and expecting to be transported to the foothills of Dunn's River Falls. So why the fuss?

But modern outrage stories are just like London Tubes. It doesn't really matter if you miss one, there'll be another arriving shortly (and it will be just as overcrowded as the last). And as the Summer of Jerk Rice was getting under way, the Twitterati turned on the American retail chain Target for daring to stock some quirky cards on Father's Day.

The cards depicted a black couple and featured the African American idiom 'Baby Daddy' on the front. No big deal, right? Wrong! There was a baby-mama-shaped frenzy on the horizon. The first customer to speak out online was Texas local Takeisha Saunders, who posted a picture of the card on Facebook with the caption: 'You CANNOT be serious Target!!!! Really!!!?!!!!? This was the only Father's Day card that featured a black couple!!!!!! #OurVoices Really #NotMyNarrative #HowAboutHusband #How AboutLove #HowAboutJustDad.'

The social media busybodies followed suit, calling 'baby daddy' a derogatory term synonymous with absent fathers, deadbeat dads and unwed parents, with many claiming that this sort of categorisation was damaging to black fathers. Good grief, is this really what we're doing?

I thought. Placing race perception in the hands of a budget department store?

Had any of the outrage bandwagoners bothered to read the words printed on the inside of the card they would have seen that it celebrated the lucky recipient as 'a wonderful husband and father'. It was hardly a banner for racial insensitivity. But sure enough, the absurdity ensued, gaining momentum with blanket coverage across the national press until the inevitable removal of the product from all Target shelves.

Because of course, the biggest problem in America in 2018 was greeting cards.

Often we lend this performative fury to the downright pointless. There were the Canadian pothole protests of 2006, where a dozen residents stood naked in their town's potholes to highlight their road-paving problems, eventually turning it into an annual calendar shoot. There was the Cornell College 'cry in' of 2016, where more than fifty university students gathered to 'hold each other, cry and hug' in collective consolation following the presidential election. And of course, the absolutely ridiculous 'austerity lunch' fiasco of 2018, which erupted when St Paul's, a private school in West London, attempted to teach its affluent students about poverty…

PRIVATE GIRLS' SCHOOL SLAMMED FOR SERVING AUS-TERITY DAY LUNCH OF JACKET POTATOES, read the *Metro* news headline. POSH PRIVATE SCHOOL SPARKS ROW WITH CRASS 'AUSTERITY DAY' LUNCH PROMOTION, wrote the *Daily Record*. MP David Lammy, whose name is never far from a spot of outrage, tweeted: 'Austerity Day? Is this a sick joke @StPaulsGirls_? A million people having to rely on food banks are not laughing! Yet another reminder of the tale of two cities we seem to be living in.' Poverty activist and food blogger Jack Monroe called the lunch stunt 'enormously patronising' in an interview with *BBC News*, adding: 'I do not know anyone who lives in poverty who can afford to turn their oven on for two hours to cook a jacket potato.'

WOULD YOU LISTEN TO YOURSELVES? People were using their valuable time, actual hours out of their day, to argue about one school's choice to serve root vegetables.

Frankly, I still don't know what all the fuss was about. So what if a £25,000-a-year school wanted to trade confit duck for baked beans and give little Beatrice and Clementine a taste of reality. It's not like they were going on work-experience placements as Georgian chimney sweeps. It was a sodding lunch.

Which brings me to the epidemic of activist absurdism. There's the Clandestine Insurgent Rebel Clown Army, a left-wing legion of clowns seeking to tackle global issues one water pistol at a time. The Swiss hippies who fought tirelessly to criminalise the boiling of live lobsters because it hurts their feelings. There were even the furious protestors that slammed 'Kimono Wednesday' at the Boston Museum of Fine Arts as 'Orientalism' and 'appropriation' after curators invited visitors to wear a kimono and pose for pictures beside Claude Monet's *La Japonaise* in 2015.

'Asian-Americans in this country have a history of being mis- or underrepresented – they're either completely absent from the media or only depicted as Kung Fu, exoticized, mystical, dragon ladies, prostitutes, or what have you,' said Christina Wang, one of the protestors quoted in the *Boston Globe*.* 'This event that the MFA is putting on – asking the public to come don the kimono – is part of that legacy.' There were picket signs including: 'Decolonize our museums' and 'Try on the kimono, learn what it's like to be a racist imperialist!!!' as well as a 'Stand Against Yellow Face' protest group on Facebook, which currently hosts more than 400 supporting members.

Look, it is impossible to rationalise an experience that isn't your own, so no, it is not my place to determine whether 'Kimono Wednesdays' warranted an outpouring of anger from Japanese Americans. Just like it's not up to Jamie Oliver to wade in on the legitimacy of #Jerkgate. So if you choose to find offence in the celebratory costuming of an art exhibit rather than say, the worrying statistic that Asian American white-collar professionals are the least likely racial group to be promoted into management roles, then so be it.

---

* 'MFA backs down over kimono event in response to protests', Malcolm Gay, *Boston Globe*, 7 July 2015. https://www.bostonglobe.com/lifestyle/style/2015/07/07/mfa-backs-down-over-kimono-event-response-protests/lv9NHcnpWolsRE77d9hvkI/story.html

5

THE WRATH OF THE RETWEET

OK, OK, *OK*! I can hear you objecting that hashtag movements *can* be important, so yes, this clicktivism intervention does indeed come with a caveat. Viral activism can have its uses by mobilising outrage and making resistance both visible and accessible for a number of worthwhile causes.

#MuteRKelly is a movement that emerged in late 2017 amidst mounting sexual-abuse accusations against disgraced R&B singer R. Kelly. It provided a course of action for thousands of people who didn't consider themselves activists but simply wanted vigilante justice to prevail where law enforcement had not. The hashtag offered an objective to what had previously been stifled outrage and subdued whispers in an entertainment industry that had never quite managed to convincingly 'cancel' the singer. #MuteRKelly acted as a way of shaming those industry gatekeepers who continued to support the singer despite widespread reports of his disturbing misconduct, eventually resulting in the cancellation of his concerts, the removal of his music from streaming playlists and the breakdown of his professional relationships. The hashtag moved offline and became a real-world protest, even courting the endorsement of #TimesUp, a movement that dwarfed #MuteRKelly despite launching months later, but that undoubtedly contributed to the accelerated unravelling of Kelly's career. By 2019 R. Kelly had been dropped by his record label Sony Music and was finally arrested on federal charges of sex trafficking and abuse.

There was #Women2Drive, a campaign that pushed new legislation over the line in Saudi Arabia, where women were not allowed to drive until 2018; the #MeToo movement, a social-justice campaign against sexual harassment and assault, which continues to empower victims around the world to speak out against their abusers; and of course #BlackLivesMatter – an era-defining movement that spread across continents in 2014 and went on to become a slogan for a new era of civil rights activism.

So yes, a collective takedown through clicktivism does have its uses.

But what if retweet culture is part of a new mob rule that is slowly killing our free will?

In the age of the retweet, hashtags often make decisions for us. Instead of generating our own views we can simply regurgitate someone else's. That digital ditto lets us bandwagon ideas rather than forming our own. In our abundantly digital era, we are falling into line without a second thought, and at times abandoning thought altogether.

Consider this for a second: if you had told an adult of sound mind to stick their head in a hot oven back in the eighties they would have told you to go fuck yourself, but here in the twenty-first century you can call it the #HotOvenChallenge and you'll have people queuing up to singe their eyebrows off for the amusement of their seventy-nine followers.

A true watershed moment for clicktivism happened back in January 2015, creating a social media moment that would perhaps define the limitations of online outrage. You might even remember where you were at the time. I certainly do. It was early in the afternoon and I'd just finished a midweek workout. I was a few days into my short-lived health kick (a New Year's resolution cliché I'd embarked on in January 2015) and like any gym rookie I was taking mirror pics in the changing room, foolishly expecting to see immediate results. It was while I was on my phone that I saw the news that Islamic extremists had burst into the offices of the French satirical magazine *Charlie Hebdo* and opened fire on their staff, killing twelve. About an hour after the attack, the slogan #JeSuisCharlie was posted on Twitter.

For those who struggled with Key Stage 3 French, 'Je Suis Charlie' translates as 'I Am Charlie'. A statement of resistance and a show of solidarity with the staff members and police officers who lost their lives to terrorism, the hashtag was used as an obstinate defence of free speech. It grew into one of the most popular Twitter moments in history, with over 6 million users attaching the hashtag to their posts within a week. It remained at the forefront of our collective conscience for weeks, with the hashtag routinely attached to an assortment of outraged Twitter posts around the world. It was written into an episode of *The Simpsons*, worn as a motto on Italy's Serie A football jerseys, projected onto French embassies and even became the name of a public square in France.

This overnight rise to fame thrust the magazine into the global spotlight, taking it from cult to mainstream. Their post-massacre edition carrying the headline JE SUIS CHARLIE became a collector's item, with asking prices of over €100,000 on eBay. The publication received a donation from Google rumoured to be in the region of $300,000 and sales of the magazine surged to 7 million copies.

But what had motivated us to share the hashtag so furiously? It wasn't the carefully considered brainchild of some trailblazing freedom fighter; it was an impulsively composed slogan written by a magazine art director who had never actually bought a copy of *Charlie Hebdo*,* itself a frequent source of outrage, offending whoever it could whenever it could. Sitting somewhere between *Viz* and *The Onion*, the magazine's radical absurdism could at times make *South Park* look like *Sesame Street*. Its extensive back catalogue of controversial images included a depiction of the Holy Trinity in a threesome, a black minister of justice as a monkey and the Prophet Muhammad carrying a bomb in his turban. The latter in this egregious trilogy in fact led to a 2007 lawsuit filed by the Grand Mosque of Paris and the French Union of Islamic Organisations. Eight years later it led to a bloodbath.

So what was it about #JeSuisCharlie that had us falling in line without hesitation?

Maybe you're an optimistic believer in the power of individual thought. You'd *never* follow the crowd, right? Well

---

* 'How the World Was Changed by the Slogan "Je Suis Charlie"', Mukul Devichand, BBC Trending, 3 January 2016. https://www.bbc.co.uk/news/blogs-trending-35108339

allow me to shit all over your affirmations of volition with the famous Asch Experiment, a study in conformity that makes for pretty grim reading.

It was conducted in 1951 by Solomon Asch, a Polish psychologist who wanted to investigate the extent to which social influence can force us to conform. Fifty male participants from Swarthmore College in Pennsylvania were placed into fifty separate engineered groups, where all the other members had been instructed to give the same wrong answer. The test was to see whether the subject, who answered second-to-last, would go against his instincts by repeating the same incorrect response he had heard from the others.

The pivotal question wasn't complicated or ambiguous. It had a clear right and wrong answer. It simply required the participants to match up one of three drawn lines of different lengths to a target line. Six-year-olds hopped up on fizzy drinks could have aced it without breaking a sweat. Yet here were fifty college students abandoning their free will in favour of the shared (and obviously wrong) answer a depressing *one out of three times*. (Over in the control group, where no coercive pressure was applied, fewer than 1 per cent of the participants gave wrong answers.)

If adults can abandon their individual power of thought when deciding something as clear-cut as the length of a line, then what might we do when the options aren't so obvious? It really is a miracle that society hasn't completely imploded yet.

Various assessments of Asch's soul-destroying experiment found that people tend to bow to social pressure for two distinct reasons. The first of these is something called 'normative influence', which is motivated by our need to fit in and our fear of rejection. The second is 'informational influence', our belief that the group knows more than we do. And sure, you're probably still reading this thinking you would have never fallen for it, but I beg to differ. Have you ever nodded when you didn't quite grasp the topic of discussion? Laughed at a joke that went over your head? Bought a sandwich because it was the last one with a particular filling left on the shelf and therefore presumably the yummiest, since everybody else went for it? We claim to be in charge of our own destiny when in reality we can barely take charge of an M&S meal deal.

Some interpretations of the Asch Experiment show that we use the judgements of others to help us form our own opinions. Others suggest that our susceptibility to outside influences increases with the size of the peer group, meaning that while we may not side with one or two cohorts, we are far more inclined to align ourselves with an entire network.

In a political context, this is what John Stuart Mill called 'the tyranny of the majority' – the persuasive power of the governing masses at the expense of individual expression. And in the digital world we are ever more pliable under the gaze of public opinion. By its very design, where random musings are sorted into a chronological sequence of posts, social media invites us to fall in line, to follow suit and stay on topic. We are living in the Era of Coercion, in which 'influencer' is an actual job title. And when we're online, as Colding-Jørgensen proved with the Stork Fountain, we are habitual conformists, willing to follow the crowd off a cliff. We don't fact-check or question. We repost and agree.

Hashtags in response to breaking news stories are like social experiments in groupthink – a term coined by social psychologist Irving Janis in the seventies (a decade defined by the mass conformity of cults, protests and polyester jumpsuits) to explain the psychological phenomenon of shared judgement and its impact on our decision-making. They provide us with an outrage stencil within which our views are supposed to fit, a cookie-cutter belief system that absolves us of any obligation to think for ourselves. We hinge entire conversations on them and regulate our responses to comply with universal opinion. Hashtags demand our compliance and offer no alternative.

So we willingly pretend, feigning offence for the sake of conformity. And this is where groupthink begins its social conditioning. For when a hashtag campaign like #JeSuisCharlie captures the vocal majority it sets a parameter around an accepted set of views, turning Twitter into a playground for vigilante legislators, where anyone who dares to contradict those values must face the wrath of social-justice warriors with their twelve-tweet-threads and Facebook dissertations.

I mean, look at what happened when French actress Catherine Deneuve denounced the #MeToo movement and its French equivalent #BalanceTonPorc (which, incredibly, translates to the far catchier 'call out your pig') by signing an open letter that read:

The Harvey Weinstein scandal sparked a legitimate awakening about the sexual violence that women are subjected to, particularly in their professional lives, where some men abuse their power. This was necessary. But what was supposed to liberate voices has now been turned on its head: We are being told what is proper to say and what we must stay silent about – and the women who refuse to fall into line are considered traitors, accomplices!

CATHERINE DENEUVE SAYS MEN SHOULD BE 'FREE TO HIT ON WOMEN' read the headlines. She was parodied on *Saturday Night Live* and dragged through the alleyways of Twitter. All for daring to decry a hashtag. She became the scapegoat of non-conformity, a poster child for misanthropy. She was berated as some sort of self-hating female chauvinist for daring to have an opinion by the same holier-than-thou feminists who, ironically, claimed to advocate for strong-willed women. Catherine Deneuve had inadvertently become the new outrage trend while trying to challenge the rationale of another one.

'Very disturbing statement by French actress Catherine Deneuve. Normalizing sexual harassment is dangerous and irresponsible. Shame on her and the people who support this. You are part of the problem. #metoo #BalanceTonPorc,' said one Twitter user.

'I doubt #CatherineDeneuve would be jumping to the defence of harassers if she weren't living in a bubble of white, wealthy, privileged, cis womanhood,' was the contribution from another.

'FUCK YOU, CATHERINE, WE'RE GOING TO ASK MEN TO TREAT YOU WITH KINDNESS AND PROFESSIONAL RESPECT WHETHER YOU LIKE IT OR NOT,' shouted *Harper's Bazaar*'s political editor from her Twitter profile @JenAshleyWright (notching up an impressive 13.2k likes.)

The following week, battered and bruised by popular opinion, Catherine Deneuve apologised for her involvement in the open letter – a U-turn that epitomised the stronghold of groupthink and our reluctance to challenge it.

Hashtag movements like #MeToo and #JeSuisCharlie position themselves on the honourable side of outrage and, in so doing, pressure us to fall in line. We watch the world tweeting along and suddenly wonder whether staying silent makes us seem complicit with the perpetrators: *If I don't join the #MeToo conversation I'll look like a sex-pest sympathiser. If I don't say 'I'm Charlie' they'll think I'm on the side of terrorism.* The Internet has become a global tyrant, enforcing new boundaries as and when it pleases. And in a world in which trending topics become political agendas and hashtags become rules, we cannot discount the number of people who are simply compelled to agree.

#JeSuisCharlie forced us to make a decision – did we stand with the slaughtered victims and in doing so endorse their freedom to blaspheme and ridicule entire religions and races, or were we on the side of the terrorists? This is not to say that the victims were not deserving of our sympathy and outrage – and acts of terrorism must be condemned – but that our outrage deserved some consideration of its own. We had every right to be furious, but had we assessed why? Were we outraged by the act of terror? By its attempt to silence the free press? By the flagrant disregard for life and liberty? Did we consider the issues that arise when a publication disguises a dissenting agenda as quick-witted and progressive? Or the messy history of French colonialism?

Or did we simply fall in line, repost and agree?

As Roxane Gay wrote in a piece provocatively entitled 'If *je ne suis pas Charlie*, am I a bad person?',* 'demands for solidarity can quickly turn into demands for groupthink, making it difficult to express nuance. It puts the terms of our understanding of the situation in black and white – you are either with us or against us – instead of allowing people to mourn and be angry while also being sympathetic to complexities that are being overlooked.'

So we were gonna be Charlie whether we *parle le Français* or not.

Many of *Charlie Hebdo*'s staunch defenders argued that the magazine was simply a daring send-up of politics that was often 'misinterpreted' by its critics. You were supposed to believe that it was being satirically homophobic by calling two women 'Old Dykes' on its cover so that we could all laugh at the farcicality of intolerance. UMMMM… I'll pass.

'There is a very narrow edge between dangerous buffoonery and freedom of expression,' said Vladimir Putin in response to the *Charlie Hebdo* attack. 'Did those cartoonists need to offend Islamic believers?'

And while I'm not one to side with Putin, the question remains… Did they?

---

* 'If *je ne suis pas Charlie*, am I a bad person? Nuance gets lost in groupthink', Roxane Gay, *Guardian*, 12 January 2015. https://www.theguardian.com/commentisfree/2015/jan/12/je-ne-suis-pas-charlie-nuance-groupthink

6

RAGE AGAINST THE MACHINE

Shortly before I started this book, when my son was almost eight months old, a friend of mine shared an infuriating article in our WhatsApp group. It was a column published in the *Daily Mail* in which serial shitwit Richard Littlejohn had waded in on the subject of same-sex parenting.

'Please don't pretend two dads is the new normal,' he began in a tirade prompted by the news that the Olympic diver Tom Daley was having a baby with his husband Dustin Lance Black. He claimed that the baby announcement was a 'publicity stunt' and said 'children benefit most from being brought up by a man and a woman'. He went on: 'Why are so many of my fellow journalists taking stuff like this at face value? Are they all afraid of asking awkward questions, lest they are monstered by the deranged diversity bigots on Twitter? Can they please grow a pair – if that's not too "transphobic" – and stop pretending this is the new normal. Not in our house, it isn't. Nor, I suspect, in yours or 99.99 per cent of the rest of the world, either.'

But while I and the other three members of our WhatsApp group were flapping around putting our outrage to very little use, there was an organisation preparing to take action. This was a collective of social media vigilantes called Stop Funding Hate and its response to Littlejohn's article was the first I heard about the work they were doing.

Stop Funding Hate is an online pressure group hoping to do just that, by starving outrage-mongers of their financial resources. Much like depriving your garden weeds of sunlight before watching them die a slow and painful death. They are doing this by encouraging what they call 'responsible advertising' and applying moral pressure to companies that pay for ad space in the likes of the *Sun* and, worse still, the campaign's arch-nemesis the *Daily Mail*.

I wondered if they might offer some tips on how we could all become more energised and effective ragers, and a few keystrokes later I found myself on Stop Funding Hate's teal-coloured webpage that looks starkly clinical, like those medical sites that let you self-assess your symptoms before inevitably diagnosing everything as bowel cancer. After navigating impatiently through their menu options (their 'contact us' page is hidden frustratingly at the bottom of a drop-down list the length of my leg), I eventually landed on an email address and, within a day, one of their co-founders, Richard Wilson, had kindly agreed to a series of phone conversations.

Richard's approach to outrage, I'd soon discover, is a world away from the furore that often accompanies hashtag movements and the mud-slinging that comes with person-to-person Twitter combat. A former Amnesty International campaigner, he began Stop Funding Hate as a one-man crusade in 2016 to which he dedicated a few hours a day (he now heads up a crowd-funded team of twelve). He speaks in short, purposeful sentences, and never raises his voice above thirty decibels. He doesn't go off on tangents or wax lyrical about morality. He's like one of those *there's no 'I' in team* guys you find at corporate team-building events, I think, as he starts to explain his ambitious strategy of cleaning up the press.

So how exactly do they plan to bring down the media's most notorious purveyors of hatred? I wondered.

'There's loads of different ways,' he says in a measured tone that convinces me he wears his hair in a side parting, 'but by far the most effective thing is if there's a particularly nasty example [of an article] on a particular day, we'll tweet with a screenshot to the brand in question. Either the one that's near it or that's advertising on the same day in the same paper and basically just confront them with it. Not in an aggressive way, just a nudge like, *Are you sure you want to be associated with this?*'

Ahhh, screenshots! Those irreversible digital receipts captured at the touch of a button. A smartphone's secret weapon. I know them well. They have ended relationships, halted careers and now, thanks to Stop Funding Hate, they're chipping away at the outrage industry.

Stop Funding Hate has successfully convinced brands including Lego and the Body Shop to permanently withdraw advertising from the *Daily Mail*, Richard tells me, but it wasn't until February 2018, when they called out the *Mail* on its alleged homophobia, that Stop Funding Hate really started shaking the table. While I was losing my shit in a private group chat, Stop Funding Hate had assembled like school prefects in a rowdy hallway to actually do something about it.

'We targeted the online advertisers and basically took loads of screenshots of whoever was advertising on that article,' Richard explained. 'We racked up dozens of different brands that were all on this one article and loads of people got tweeting.'

I wondered why Richard doesn't target readers of the outrage press too. 'Aren't they also funding hate?' I propose. His answer is locked and loaded, suggesting that he's perhaps had to shoot down nonsense notions like this before.

'The *Sun* are selling 1.4 million copies a day, which is a significant number, but there's 65 million people in the UK,' he points out. 'It's a tiny proportion of the population that is going out and buying the paper on any given day, but almost all of us will be shopping with a company that advertises with them. So in terms of actually being effective and having an impact, it's not that we don't think it's relevant to talk to the readers, but there is a much larger pool of people who are helping to pay for this through the advertising.'

For Richard, it is the financial lifelines funding the sale of hate and outrage that need to be held accountable in order for us to have any chance at collapsing this malign empire. 'For a very long time,' he explains, 'there was almost a rule that companies would say: *It's not our place to make a judgement about the editorial content. We're just gonna turn up and give them the money for the advertising.* What we are arguing is there needs to be a recognition that you do have some responsibility for what you're funding as an advertiser and you can't wash your hands of the moral consequences, especially if those moral consequences include people being attacked in the streets and subjected to real extremes of behaviour as a consequence of that hate. So if we can get to a point where companies recognise that they've got a moral responsibility to think about this stuff and then make their advertising choices accordingly, that could be completely transformative.'

He tells me: 'Digital advertising alone is $200 billion a year and rising.' (I later Google this and, astonishingly, the annual digital advertising spend is expected to reach $384.96 billion worldwide in 2020 and has been eclipsing TV advertising since 2017). 'Even if 10 per cent of that money was redirected away from the media outlets that create hatred and towards the many others that are doing a really good job, then you've got the opportunity there for really big systemic change, because ultimately we want to make hate unprofitable.'

Making hate unprofitable sounds like a utopian dream, but one that feels oddly achievable the more I speak to Richard. This isn't just a bunch of Twitter users getting in an aimless flap; it is a strategic takedown of a perilous system.

So what is the end goal in their peaceful (yet strategically savage) approach of holding brands publicly accountable?

'There's two levels to it,' he tells me, in a rising tone. 'The immediate goal is to get to the point where we're just not seeing racist, hateful, divisive, anti-trans, homophobic stories in mainstream UK newspapers any more. A UK press that's free from discrimination...' He pauses. 'To get there we've got to try and bring about a cultural change in the way that big companies think about their advertising.'

According to Richard, twelve companies pulled their advertising in the days that followed their response to the Littlejohn column, a feat that he calls their most 'outstanding' result to date. The campaign continued to challenge the likes of NatWest, Honda, Boots Pharmacy, Suzuki, Morrisons and Iceland (the frozen food store, not the Nordic island), he tells me with a hint of pride. Center Parcs tweeted, 'We take where we advertise very seriously and have a number of steps to prevent our advertising from appearing alongside inappropriate content. We felt this placement was completely unacceptable and therefore ceased advertising with the *Daily Mail* with immediate effect.'

Eventually, the *Daily Mail* responded with a statement in the *Press Gazette*:

> Had any of the political zealots who attacked Richard Littlejohn's column actually read it they would know that he explicitly supports civil partnerships and the fostering of children by gay couples – hardly evidence of homophobia. Nor is it homophobic to ask whether it is right to deny a child the love of its own mother. It is very sad that an advertiser should give way to bullying by a tiny group of politically motivated Internet trolls in their attempts to censor newspapers with which they disagree.

Interestingly, adverts on Littlejohn columns are now completely non-existent. Richard's strategy has earned him the trust of a few whistle-blowers, he tells me. 'We've actually had more than one case of people who have recently left one of the papers who have then got in touch with us to offer useful advice. Even people who have worked for them have perhaps been a bit unsettled by what they were a part of.' He laughs cagily. 'Almost all of it comes with the caveat: *please don't tell anyone I've talked to you* – so I shouldn't say more than that,' he adds.

Surely, then, he is public enemy number one among his media targets. Isn't he even slightly worried that he'll end up buried in a shallow grave in Epping Forest? 'The *Mail*, the *Sun* and the *Express* have all publicly attacked us,' he tells me when I ask whether the press now have a personal vendetta against him. 'You can find some pretty extreme stuff personally attacking all of us.'

And he wasn't lying. It didn't take me long to find a full-page spread in the *Daily Mail* hitting out at him after Stop Funding Hate had successfully lobbied the stationery chain Paperchase against advertising in the paper. Four days earlier, the retailer had run a wrapping-paper giveaway in the *Mail*'s Saturday edition. By 10 a.m. @stopfundinghate had tweeted: 'After a torrid few weeks of divisive stories about trans people, is a *Daily Mail* promotion really what customers want to see @FromPaperchase? #StartSpreadingLove #StopFundingHate.'

Customers wasted no time weighing in: 'Paperchase is normally first stop when Christmas shopping. But for as long as you're in the *Daily Mail*, it's on my naughty list.' Another added: 'Paperchase must realise the *Mail* actively promotes xenophobia/homophobia/anti-women/Islamophobia, and your advertising partnership implies you share these views, or do not see their hate promotion as significant enough to oppose. Please consider what this says about your brand.'

On Monday morning, Paperchase, evidently panicking as their lucrative festive season approached, released the following online statement:

We've listened to you about this weekend's newspaper promotion. We now know we were wrong to do this – we're truly sorry and we won't ever do it again. Thanks for telling us what you really think and we apologise if we have let you down on this one. Lesson learnt.

The next day, *Sunday Times* deputy editor Sarah Baxter appeared on *Newsnight* claiming that Paperchase were 'a company being bullied by a small army of Twitter and social media trolls into using activism as a weapon against the free press'. talkRadio host and Brexiteer Julia Hartley-Brewer called the response from Paperchase an 'absurd grovelling apology' and threatened to boycott the retailer in retaliation.

On Wednesday, the *Daily Mail* responded in an article titled: MEDIA MUST DO WHAT WE WANT, SAYS ACTIVIST WHO ATTACKED FIRM OVER ITS PROMOTION IN THE MAIL, referring to the Stop Funding Hate board as 'hard Left pro-Remain Corbynistas seeking to suppress legitimate debate'. The *Mail* writers got into formation with what they probably hoped would be a synchronised takedown of Stop Funding Hate and over on page seventeen columnist Sarah Vine called the campaigners an 'arrogant, tiny minority who want to impose their views on us all'.

Writing in the *Sun*, then Foreign Secretary Boris Johnson added: 'The misleadingly named "Stop Funding Hate" campaign wants to shut down those whose views they dislike – an aim which should outrage all who care about freedom of expression,'* he wrote, conceding that, 'It is deeply disturbing to learn that this campaign is beginning to have an effect.'

I asked Richard about free speech and whether he felt that his campaign was eroding constitutional rights by imposing moral censorship.

'We don't want to get bogged down in an argument about it,' he starts, 'but free speech is like the free market: it doesn't exist in a bubble. If you don't have a government enforcing the rule of law, nobody has free speech because anyone could just come and beat you up for what you say.'

I listen intently, sensing that we're about to land somewhere important.

'Sometimes people think of free speech a bit like Fight Club – the only rule is there are no rules,' he says (making a complete hash of the Brad Pitt quote; there are in fact eight rules of Fight Club). 'But, actually, for free speech to exist people need security, people need protection, people need to not be subjected to threats,' he continues. 'If a Muslim woman can't walk down the road wearing whatever clothes she wants to wear because of hatred that is being incited against them, then they don't have freedom of expression. So our argument actually would be, if you want free speech for everybody, you do have to draw some red lines. You have to prevent threats, you have to prevent hate speech, you have to prevent the incitement of hatred, because the culture of hatred actually silences people who are being targeted.'

---

* 'Leftie activists trying to silence newspapers they dislike are attacking the very basis of our democracy', Boris Johnson, *Sun*, 5 December 2017. https://www.thesun.co.uk/news/5075450/boris-johnson-stop-funding-hate-pizza-hut/

I take a breath, preparing to ask my next question, but apparently he isn't done.

'It's more of a nuanced way of thinking about how free speech really works in practice,' he continues. 'I think no one is really a free-speech absolutist; there is almost no one in the world who could reasonably say there should never be a limit on what can be printed. For example, you can't print state secrets. You can't infringe copyright; people are always suing each other for libel. You can lose hundreds of thousands of pounds for telling lies about people. Is anyone gonna say, "Let's get rid of all the libel laws?" What about children's medical records? In reality there are all these things, which are already commonly agreed red lines that have to be protected.'

Perhaps there will, one day, be a legal intervention preventing the dissemination of outrage, forcing media outlets to exercise a duty of care, but until then we have to police our own responses. 'We need to realise the power we have as consumers when we get together,' Richard says, pointing out the cultural shift that's needed. And I suspect he's right. If Stop Funding Hate could teach us anything it is that there is more power in a common goal than there is in individual impulses. It is strength in numbers that allows Stop Funding Hate to force the hand of corporate giants. So what did Richard actually think of mass outrage?

'It depends how it's channelled,' he says, adding that it only works 'when there is a purpose to it and it's pro-portionate'. He points out that while Stop Funding Hate's vehicle for change *is* outrage it isn't 'vehement vitriol'.

'There's another way that this can play out,' he goes on. 'We're always seeing comments from people who just really hate Richard Littlejohn and they really hate Katie

Hopkins, they hate them personally and they wish them ill. We see the most horrible comments and actually we think that's counterproductive, because you're feeding the machine. You're getting sucked in by the forces of nastiness.'

He doesn't want to sound pious, he says, though there is something undeniably saintly about his approach. 'When our side personalises it and throws hate back, it actually undermines the idea of rising above hate,' he adds, with the mystifying evangelism of a church vicar. 'The other thing is realising that we can be a part of the problem as well, and almost vowing not to get sucked in ourselves and not to be a part of it,' he says. 'So don't send that angry tweet to that columnist; just ignore that columnist. Don't give them the attention, don't give them the outrage and the hatred that they crave. Don't be part of the machine. If enough people just say I'm not gonna play this game any more, I'm not gonna get sucked in, I'm not gonna get angry, then the machine won't work any more because we're not feeding it.'

When the buyer becomes savvier than the enterprise, the business goes bust.

7

OUTRAGE FATIGUE

Speaking to Richard at Stop Funding Hate had made it clearer than ever to me just how pointless mass outrage is when it isn't channelled into any measurable purpose. If those guys could get half the British press shaking in their brown-leather brogues, why couldn't all protest be as effective? I mean, here we are pouring our outrage into the dragging of brands and all we're usually compensated with is a carefully worded 'sorry'.

Picture Steve in public relations at DumbAd Inc. on a lowly salary of 20k a year, composing draft number twenty-seven of an earnest and heartfelt retraction of an 'insensitive' and 'misjudged' advert on behalf of the company that wouldn't even give him two weeks paternity leave. His superiors keep circulating emails with eight other people cc'd telling him to make it 'more sincere' and 'less grovelling'. Poor Steve probably said the ad was a crap idea in the first place. But the board of directors finally signs off on draft thirty-eight. Steve, who hates his job, goes home to his exasperated wife, and the embarrassing statement of regret makes its way onto our timelines.

Yes, this is how the story usually ends. First comes the mass outrage then comes the eye-roll-inducing apology.

Pepsi was trying to project a global message of unity, peace and understanding. Clearly we missed the mark, and we apologize. We did not intend to make light of any serious issue. We are removing the content and halting any further rollout. We also apologize for putting Kendall Jenner in this position. – Pepsi

An image we recently posted on Facebook missed the mark in representing women of color thoughtfully. We deeply regret the offence it caused. – Dove

We realise that we missed the mark with this messaging. We have removed this messaging from all future marketing materials. We fully support our community in loving their bodies and feeling confident in their own skin. – Avon

Gucci deeply apologises for the offence caused by the wool balaclava jumper. We consider diversity to be a fundamental value to be fully upheld, respected, and at the forefront of every decision we make. – GUCCI

We want to apologise if we have made mistakes in interpreting your culture. We have always loved China; we have visited many cities and certainly we still have much to learn. We offer our sincerest apologies to Chinese people worldwide. – Dolce & Gabbana

Food allergies are a serious issue. Our film should not have made light of Peter Rabbit's arch-nemesis, Mr McGregor, being allergic to blackberries, even in a cartoonish, slapstick way. – Sony Pictures

Krispy Kreme apologises unreservedly for the inappropriate name of a customer promotion at one of our stores. We are truly sorry for any offence this completely unintentional oversight may have caused. – Krispy Kreme (after receiving backlash for 'KKK Wednesdays' a detestable acronym for Krispy Kreme Klub)

We throw our #KanyeWestIsCancelled parties and slap each other on the back as if 'sorry' is some monumental win for morality, convinced that we are humanity's great crusaders while jostling for front-row seats at the next big walk of shame. But the truth is, my loves, *apologies don't mean SHIT*.

Yes, I agree that it's fun to kick big corporations in the dick and there are few things more satisfying than a snivelling plea for mercy, but when someone is backed into a corner, holding their hands up and pleading for forgiveness, outrage no longer has a purpose. The bloodthirsty sport of public dragging needs some degree of opposition in order for it to work, because outrage, even the frivolous variety, is rooted in resistance. It seeks to oppose, to tackle and to hold accountable. This cannot be achieved if the wrongdoers have already chastised themselves.

Brands, as well as politicians, TV personalities and obnoxious YouTubers, have all learned that they can evade outrage with carefully considered U-turns. A convincing (even if disingenuous) display of regret can go a long way to salvage a career. In fact, brands can now be strategically and intentionally tone-deaf in exchange for some temporary notoriety, safe in the knowledge that the slate can be wiped clean with some well-orchestrated take-backs. (Yes, I'm talking about you, GBK.)*

And once a brand has said sorry, it is business as usual. If not better.

In the year that Target were on the receiving end of mass fury over their Father's Day card, they went on to record an annual sales increase of 5 per cent (their strongest revenue performance since 2005) and returned $951 million to shareholders at the end of the following year. Two months after Pepsi apologised for their Kendall Jenner ad crisis, the beverage giants reported a revenue increase of 2 per cent to $15.7 billion for the same quarter.

Even H&M survived the hoody debacle with their reputation and revenue intact. After eight days of unrelenting outrage, the furore had died down entirely. The boycotts subsided, the angry tweets dried up, radio phone-ins moved on and the opinion pieces dwindled into the obscurity of page six on Google. By the end of the year, the high street fashion chain was celebrating an online sales increase of 22 per cent and, I imagine, an impressive surge in brand awareness.

Come to think of it, considering how many of my friends were 'outraged' by the retailer back in 2018, I'm baffled by the number of H&M T-shirts they still seem to be buying my son on his birthdays.

---

* In 2018 after a tough financial year, British restaurant chain Gourmet Burger Kitchen decided to dabble in outrage marketing with the Ruby Murray burger – a bap filled with spiced lamb, samosa relish and a poppadum, an (admittedly yummy-sounding) embodiment of cultural appropriation. They provocatively declared that the burger was 'proper Indian' food before foolishly deciding that the best way to launch it was with a PR stunt that showed a white GBK representative heckling customers outside real Indian restaurants. GBK eventually apologised for their ad campaign, but kept the burger on the menu.

So eighteen months after I'd abandoned my family holiday to write the article that had been triggered by monkeygate, I decided to get in touch with the blogger who had started it, Stephanie Yeboah, known online as @NerdAboutTown. I had spoken to some of the subjects of our outrage, I realised, but not to any instigators of it. Every moment of mass fury has to start with somebody, I thought, and I was now incredibly curious to know what it felt like to lead a digital dragging from the front.

With a head full of potential questions drowning out all my other thoughts, I excitedly sent Stephanie a direct message and a day or two later, I was listening to her slow and thoughtful voice on the phone. A dark-skinned, plus-sized influencer, Stephanie has a reputation for speaking out against offensive content and is a respected voice for body positivity. Her articulate and well-informed content had made its way onto my timeline long before I read *that* tweet in January 2018. And right from the start of our call, I knew that I liked her. She isn't at all overbearing, not in the way you'd expect of someone who had managed to whip the entire Internet into a frenzy. Quite the opposite, in fact. She is softly spoken and attentive. As we talked, I felt she was listening to understand, and not simply in order to respond.

I started by asking how she had she encountered the monkey hoodie in the first place.

She laughed. 'I was on the H&M website, buying something for my friend's son,' she said. 'I was going through all of the baby stuff and I'd already been on some other websites looking for stuff. I can't remember what I was looking for; I think it was a matching co-ord set or something. And on the side panel where they've got that thing if you're looking at one product it might have another product under "things you may like" – so it was just on the side. And I was like, *Oh, H&M are using black models, how progressive and great.* Then I clicked on it and I was like, *Oh, monkey, interesting.*'

'So what jumped out at you as offensive?'

'When I first saw the image, my first thought was like *Really?*' she said, re-enacting the moment with such exasperation I could almost see her eyes rolling. 'I didn't immediately jump to them being racist, I was more on the side of *This is utterly tone-deaf and it's very insensitive.* I didn't jump to the racism,' she said again.

'For me it was a sense of they need to start hiring more black people because they may not have seen the implications of doing this. I did see some more images from that photo shoot and there were other kids, white kids, and they all had a specific animal that they were wearing and it just so happened that the black child had the monkey. They obviously took a huge misstep and probably didn't see what they were doing. But it was a good way to say look, brands need to hire black people otherwise things like this are just gonna keep happening again and again, whether it's on purpose or not.'

She explained how she took a screenshot of five-year-old model Liam Mango in the ill-famed hoody and put it on Twitter.

'I think I wrote something like: *Why would you make this poor black baby wear the monkey.* It wasn't even an outright calling-out. I didn't go in with fire and blood and say *How dare you do this!* It was more a case of *why* would you do this?'

Her tweet read: 'Whose idea was it at @hm to have this little sweet black boy wear a jumper that says "coolest monkey in the jungle"? I mean. What.'

It has since generated more than 18,000 retweets and 26,000 likes.

I tell Stephanie that my son wears 'cheeky monkey' pyjamas and that I'd never question putting him in them. 'So did you not consider whether they didn't see it as racist because it wasn't?' I suggested.

'It's a difficult one to tread,' she replied thoughtfully. 'Would it stop me, if I had a child, giving them a jumper that said "monkey" on it? I don't know, probably not. I guess it's really difficult. I don't really know where to draw the line, because it can come across as completely innocent. I had a Christmas jumper last year that had a picture of Harambe on it,' she went on. 'A proper over-the-top cheesy Christmas jumper. I would wear it out and not think about it. But then I would get comments from people at work saying: *Oh Steph, isn't that a bit racist?* And I was like: *Well no, it's just a picture of Harambe.* But then I didn't really make the mental [connection].'

I thought back to the BBC broadcaster Danny Baker, who just a few weeks before had been fired from his Saturday morning radio show when he tweeted a picture of a chimpanzee following the birth of Prince Harry and Meghan's baby. The caption read: 'Royal baby leaves hospital.'

Whether he had been intentionally or inadvertently racist (he insists it is the latter), our modern landscape of outrage-at-all-costs meant that Baker could mitigate his dismissal by claiming that it was *us* who had gone mad. He didn't hold himself accountable, he blamed our political correctness. 'The call to fire me from @bbc5live was a masterclass of pompous faux-gravity,' he wrote on Twitter minutes after the BBC press office announced his firing. 'Took a tone that said I actually meant that ridiculous tweet and the BBC must uphold blah blah blah. Literally threw me under the bus. Could hear the suits knees knocking. #Fuckem.'

And five months into my outrage safari, scrolling down my Twitter feed, I had seen a fifteen-word post that I knew would embroil its composer in a shitstorm. I texted my agent and attached a screenshot with the message: 'This is gonna turn into one for the book.' Two minutes later the tweet had been deleted, but it was, of course, too late for that as I (and thousands of others) had already immortalised it in our camera rolls.

The offender was the business juggernaut and host of the BBC's *The Apprentice*, Lord Alan Sugar. His tweet had shown an image of the Senegal football team, edited to include handbags and sunglasses, and said: 'I recognise some of these guys from the beach in Marbella. Multi tasking resourceful chaps.'

The Twittersphere had let out a collective gasp. A paragraph of shocked face emojis wouldn't come close to how gobsmacked I was myself. Sugar was suggesting that these eleven African athletes, who, by the way, had accomplished an impressive World Cup win against Poland the previous day, were the same poverty-stricken 'looky looky' street vendors who sell cheap knock-offs on the Costa del Sol.

The 'can't you take a joke?' brigade leapt to his defence, but they were drowned out by the tsunami of outrage. There were angry calls for his dismissal and many drew comparisons with other transgressors axed by the broadcasting corporation, including the presenter Reggie Yates, fired from *Top of the Pops* after making anti-Semitic comments on a podcast, and DJ Logan Sama, sacked from Radio 1 Xtra after some racially charged tweets were brought to light. By lunchtime the bookmakers Paddy Power were already offering odds of 5/1 on Lord Sugar deleting his Twitter account in 2018 and evens on the BBC announcing that Lord Sugar would not appear on the next series of *The Apprentice*.

The verbal reprisals were warranted; the tweet was steeped in racial prejudice. It assumed the widespread belief that all black people are indistinguishable from each other, a very real issue that has led to many picture-desk blunders, legal altercations and wrongful convictions. It struggled to comprehend the capacity for upward mobility among black people, instead belittling us as subordinates within the economic system. And most significantly in this context, it relied heavily on the shared supposition that black people are subservient in society and can therefore be the butt of a 'joke' without repercussion.

I don't doubt that it would have got a resounding 'LOL' from Lord Sugar's bingo buddies in the WhatsApp group chat. But was it a hostile expression of hate, or a ridiculous moment of madness by an uneducated fossil who wrongly thought that the racial jibes commonly thrown around by his elderly peers would go down well on a social media platform used by younger and more culturally conscious voices?

Two deleted tweets and a plethora of jibes later, Lord Sugar posted a revised apology, more than likely ghostwritten by an army of panicked PRs: 'I misjudged my earlier tweet. It was in no way intended to cause offence, and clearly my attempt at humour has backfired. I have deleted the tweet and am very sorry.' And regardless of whether his tweet was malicious hate speech or a hint at early-onset dementia, we still sat down in our millions to watch Lord Sugar's fourteenth series of *The Apprentice* just four months later.

'Did you expect the mass outrage that followed your tweet?' I asked Stephanie.

'I didn't,' she said. 'It just kind of blew up. I was like, OK, let me just log off for a few minutes, because I wasn't going in with the intention of writing a full thread about H&M. Then I wrote a few sentences and kind of left it at that. Then it just took on a life of its own,' she said almost regretfully.

'The day after, I was on my way to work at the bus stop in Elephant and Castle and there was a cyclist on the part of the road closest to the bus stop and I had my headphones in but he kept staring at me. So I took my headphones out and he must have recognised me from Twitter because he said, "Are you the one that did that monkey tweet?" And I was like, Yeah. And then he called me a fat gorilla and cycled off. I just got on the first bus that arrived because I was so embarrassed that it happened in front of everyone. That was when I was like, *OK, this has gone VIRAL VIRAL.*' I winced as she recalled the moment of abuse.

'The news started calling me,' she said. 'Then you had people like Diddy and The Weeknd boycotting H&M and I was like, *Oh shit.* It got really intense ... A few days later I saw a video that came up on social media in a South

African H&M, where people had gone to raid it and were breaking the glass, tearing all the clothes off the rails. They just went in and attacked the whole store and I felt absolutely disgusted. I felt so sad because obviously it wasn't the fault of the people that worked in the store; they're just doing their job.'

I remembered the footage from a clip I'd seen on an Instagram gossip page. The video emerged five days after Stephanie's tweet and showed dozens of protestors dressed in red running riot in the East Rand Mall branch of H&M. They pulled down clothing rails, pushed over mannequins and ransacked displays in an act of outrage that seemed entirely disproportionate to Stephanie's tweet.

In truth, the outrage that followed Stephanie's tweet was far more incensed than she had ever been. She didn't make any allegations of racism or call for any action to be taken. She had simply made an observation and shared it. Sure, she was held up as the Pied Piper of the ensuing protest, but that wasn't a role she had ever asked for. 'That's it!' she exclaimed with an air of relief when I relayed my observation. 'And that's why it almost scared me, because I was like, *Guys, I'm not trying to encourage a worldwide protest here*, I was just making a throwaway comment.'

By calling out a global brand, Stephanie seemed to have found herself behind the wheel of a vehicle she had no interest in driving. I wondered then if she had ended up losing far more than a retail giant like H&M ever could have. 'The negative press was awful for H&M, but it's almost as though it impacted you just as badly on a personal level,' I said.

'It was overwhelming, to be honest,' she sighed. 'I'm glad that it got the attention it did in terms of raising awareness of the fact that there need to be more black people and people of colour within these structures of marketing and PR, but everything else that came from it just made me a bit sad and a bit overwhelmed. People were actually being really horrible about it,' she said, in a very matter-of-fact tone of voice. 'Being flat-out racist and calling me a gorilla … White men saying "You're taking this too seriously" or "It's not racist, you've got a chip on your shoulder" and "Not everything has to be about race".' (She explained that before she blocked people she would check their profile pictures to see who was replying with negative comments.)

'It was just a trifecta of nonsense, to be honest,' she said.

'Would you do it again, though?' I asked, expecting an emphatic 'no'.

'I think it's important to call people out directly. Otherwise, by us not doing it, it further facilitates white supremacy and keeps it going … I've done it in the past where a brand has genuinely seen that and said, "Oh I didn't realise my whole Instagram feed was full of white women and we're gonna try and do better next time." Then I've seen a couple months later that they've started being more inclusive and diverse … So I don't have a problem with doing stuff like that. But I think next time I just need to be a bit more careful with what I'm choosing to call out, because I think with the whole H&M thing, that kind of took on a whole case of its own.'

'Do you feel like you now have to be this spokesperson for outrage?' I asked.

'Yeah.' She paused. 'Because I tend to talk a lot about social-justice issues and race and body types on my social media, it has got to a point now where people come to me for comments on specific things. But it almost comes across as a bit insidious because it's like I'm now the go-to angry black woman and I hate that.'

She paused and sighed again, as though the whole thing had taken a toll on her. 'I think when you do become that voice for people, especially when it comes to plus-size issues and black women issues, people will start expecting you to be the voice for every single thing and that can be such a detriment on your mental health. People are expecting you to dive deep into that trauma to talk about an issue that you may not want to talk about. That's one of the things I don't like, because you can't just turn on your anger like a tap.'

I wondered if she thought I was mad for not being offended by the H&M image.

'No, I don't think you are,' she answered reassuringly. 'When you're having to navigate life being a black woman and always having these images and these things blasted at you from every angle it gets tiring... I think it's because we're so used to outwardly being attacked and having these racist micro-aggressions pointed at us that it gets to a point where we're tired and we don't care,' she continued. 'Sometimes it costs so much emotional energy to get angry that sometimes I'd rather just not.'

'I think part of why I'm so exhausted by the whole outrage machine is that quite often it doesn't go beyond tweets,' I said. 'So much of it just begins and ends on Twitter.'

'It does tend to be a social media thing only,' she agreed.
'I'm always open to hearing what brands have to say and
trying to come up with an actual solution as opposed
to just doing outrage performance on Twitter and just
leaving it at that,' she said, explaining that she didn't make
contact with H&M at the time because it had been so
overwhelming in terms of the press attention. 'I kind of
just wanted to get away from it as soon as possible because
of all the abuse I was getting,' she said. 'I wanted to be like
OK, that happened, now everyone leave me alone. It was a really
stressful time.' She sounded so despondent I worried that
I was forcing her to relive some deep-seated trauma.

Did she feel our online fury had become performative
and self-serving, I wondered.

'Oh gosh! Yeah, a lot of it is!' she said. 'Everyone is
trying to be angry all the time, everyone is trying to
call people out, everyone is trying to cancel people and
there are instances where people deserve to be cancelled, but there are instances where people just want
to create noise on Twitter because they realise that they
have the opportunity to go viral. It kind of diminishes
what the real issues are as well,' she went on. 'If people
are getting upset over every little thing, then there are
gonna be instances where real issues are seeping through
the cracks. We have to pick and choose what the real
issues are and what we can get angry at, otherwise we're
diluting the serious issues.'

I remembered something Molly Crockett had said about
our overexposure to outrage. According to Crockett, these
heightened experiences of digital shaming could alter our
moral attitudes for generations to come. She calls this

'outrage fatigue' and describes it as the long-term consequence of an increased frequency of extreme triggers. 'Constant exposure to outrageous news could diminish the overall intensity of outrage experiences, or cause people to experience outrage more selectively to reduce emotional and attentional demands,' she writes.

I mean, think about it for a second. We log in to our digital bubbles every day and are met with a constant outrage frenzy; thousands of 2D profiles engaging in the Oppression Olympics, attempting to outsuffer each other for clicks and retweets. Then, if that wasn't enough, there's also an endless conveyor belt of real injustices that we're meant to have the capacity to protest as well – school shootings, austerity, wage gaps, police brutality, elections, Brexit. Is it any wonder then that our outrage has the stamina of an asthmatic kid on Sports Day?

'Looking back, I don't even think I would have written anything, to be honest,' Stephanie told me as our call drew to an end. 'It's not every single issue that people can expect me to talk about, because I need to protect my peace as well.'

I thought back to how full of gumption Richard Wilson had sounded in his pursuit of change. Stephanie seemed so dejected in comparison. I began to wonder if she simply had it harder. The emotional resilience it takes to be resolutely outraged is perhaps easier to source if you're a middle-class white man than if you're a plus-sized, dark-skinned woman from Battersea. If it seems like Richard has all the answers, is that because he was born with access to the cheat codes? I wanted to believe that we all have the capacity to be just as resolute as each other in our outrage, but what if it isn't that simple? Could it be that there are some whose tolerance tanks have been so drained by society that they are simply too tired to fully apply themselves to a long-term cause?

Is this why we pour our energy into frivolities like monkey hoodies or Rachel Dolezal? Why we are so hung up on pointless petitions, hashtag activism and the pantomime-style villainy of people like Katie Hopkins? Are we simply tackling things that seem within reach, fearing our impotence in the face of the bigger issues? Maybe it is just easier to focus on life's trivial missteps when the real challenges feel so insurmountable. But by doing this aren't we also exhausting ourselves on petty grievances and leaving nothing in the tank for the real issues?

I wondered if I had become so desensitised by a lifetime of social unrest that constantly battling against it feels far too tedious. Because to be honest, the monotony of constant outrage bores me. Like a rent boy after a double shift at a one-room brothel on Wang Wednesdays – I am fucking tired.

8

MAKE OUTRAGE GREAT AGAIN

Short of building a free-speech bunker in my back garden for when the inevitable outrage apocalypse strikes, I have done pretty much everything imaginable to protect myself from the online mob. I've deleted Facebook, decreased the frequency of my social media commentary and all but retired from posting hot takes. I've toned down my digital temperament, sat out contentious debates and avoided fires I would quite happily have stoked in my past life as a Twitter menace.

A few months before I was due to submit the manuscript for this book I even used an online service called Tweet Delete to erase my old posts from the Internet. The website, which allows you to specify time frames or key words for posts you would like removed, launched in 2011 and has since become a go-to service for a burgeoning community of outrage evaders who wish to wipe their digital slates clean. Think of it as a contract killer for the problematic person you used to be, with optional extras available for a premium fee of $9.99.

I felt like I had enrolled myself in a witness protection programme.

So yes, I wrote this book in part out of sheer terror, that worrisome trepidation that I might, one day, wind up on the wrong end of a Twitter dig and find myself jobless. And, of course, in the hope that it could play some small part in changing the tide.

Because the pervasiveness of outrage is diluting our moral expression and weakening our moral leverage. We've regressed into a bunch of namby-pamby Saul Alinsky wannabees, in constant need of 'safe spaces' and 'account-ability'. An aimless army of hypersensitive dandelions who fall apart every time the wind blows.

ITV's *This Morning* programme recently discussed whether the phrase 'hey guys' was offensive to those who don't identify as 'guys'. I shit you not. An actual debate about whether we need a new gender-neutral greeting. A few weeks later a job post on Twitter descended into an equal rights stand-off after the employer failed to clarify whether he would consider women for a roofing vacancy. Soon after that, I read an article by a social justice war-rior insisting that the use of the word 'nude' in the beauty industry was problematic. I actually considered making a noose out of my dressing-gown cord and ending it all at this point.

The fact is this: worthwhile causes still exist. They warrant our disdain and need our attention. If you insist on being outraged, why not try some of these on for size: in South Africa, it is estimated that more than 1,000 incidents of rape occur every single day, with one in four men admitting to having sexually assaulted a woman. Or how about the fact that abortion is still illegal in more than fifty countries? Then there's the small matter of stop-and-search practices in the UK, where black people are nine times as likely as whites to be randomly checked for the possession of drugs. Add to this the fact that people of colour are more harshly sentenced than white people, or that more than 18,000 years of wrongful jail sentences have been served in America by exonerated prisoners in the last thirty years. Maybe you could also consider the 14 million young girls forced into child marriage every year, or that every year 54,000 women in the UK are permanently forced out of their jobs once they become pregnant, and I'm sure you'll concur that there are more pressing matters on the outrage agenda than Jamie Oliver's jerk rice.

In our final frontier there is still so much to be *truly* outraged by. There's the gender pay gap, racial bias, police brutality, homophobia, transphobia, misogynoir, gun control and those absolute fuckturds who think climate change is a hoax.

So by all means get angry. Get as angry as you possibly can. But do it with an ambition that extends beyond social media kudos. Because all we are doing is desensitising a generation and robbing them of their right to be effectively furious. And I don't want my son to grow up in a world where he dare not speak because hypersensitivity and outrage culture have silenced opinion. But I also don't want him to have to navigate a future where wrongdoings go without consequence because we cheapened outrage and rendered it completely ineffective.

We stand on the shoulders of true social revolutionaries, those who lived lives of real resistance. The reason we are now able to walk freely into social and political disputes, whether they be worthwhile or trivial, is because those very paths were carved out for us by the insurgents of years gone by. They afforded us the freedom to pick and choose our battles by fighting the fundamental ones so tirelessly. Women can now speak out about gender disparity because we now have a voice. Black people can now march against police brutality because the shackles have moved from our ankles to our wrists.

We have so much security that there is now the luxury of choice. We can *choose* what to be offended by, when to be offended by it and for how long we want it to offend us. So why seek out more darkness? Why navigate a route with the most obstacles?

OK, let's weigh up some harsh realities. We're all gonna die; of that we can be certain. One day there will be a funeral where you are the main attraction. And until that day comes, a ton of steaming-hot crap is gonna come your way. Debt, ill-health, maybe you'll even get blindsided by a gut-wrenching case of infidelity. Life is not your friend. Like a learner driver at a roundabout, it is gonna try your patience.

Trust me, I grit my teeth through some absolute bullshit on a daily basis. The rent-a-cop security guard who feels the sudden urge to stray from the shop entrance and start patrolling the aisles when I walk into Boots; the waitress who calls me 'sir' simply because I do not conform to the international doctrine of femininity; the utter disdain on the faces of some parents as they try to compute how on earth my son has two mums; the country bumpkins who look up in horror when I, a black, dare to stop for a roast dinner in their rural pub; the businessmen who wonder how the hell us 'coloureds' got into the Virgin Atlantic first-class lounge at Heathrow Airport.

But guess what, folks: addressing each and every encounter with ignorance isn't gonna get this mortgage paid. Being outraged by everything is simply impractical. It's like trying to single-handedly carry your whole weekly shop from the car to the front door in one trip. You're gonna have to leave some bags behind, hun.

Take me, for example. My race, sexuality and gender mean that society has at least three boots on my neck. So I could resign myself to this fact and allow my entire existence to be agitated by every insult, misstep and injustice encountered in the minefield that is gay black womanhood, or I can define myself for myself.

And I choose to be the architect of my own experience (in a world that would have me believe that the blueprints are not mine to design). I *choose* not to be excessively outraged, not out of weakness or out of some colonial submission, but because it's my goddamn prerogative.

Incessant outrage is for those who have bound themselves to a lifetime of victimhood, punctuated by daily affronts to their being. So I don't care if your phone contract includes a lifetime of free data; you work too damn hard to be wasting your hard-earned megabytes on people who insist on seeing the world differently to you. For the sake of your own self-care it is time to filter out the noise. Go outside, buy an ice cream, escape the fucking frenzy. There is only so much goading and baiting your sanity can withstand, so why not make the choice to free yourself from the outrage industry?

For when you finally decide to use your outrage spar-
ingly, you grant yourself autonomy. You free yourself from
the shackles of public opinion and reclaim your volition.
You refuse to be sorted into society's pecking order where
the power*less* are outraged and the power*ful* are serene.
Freedom from outrage is freedom from control. It sticks
a middle finger up at the capitalism of social politics and
shatters the business model of outrage-mongers. It allows
you to redirect your energy away from the performative
and towards the productive.

Resisting the urge to be outraged is fucking badass.

Of course, some people stifle their outrage because they
have jobs to keep, rent to pay or husbands to find. They
silence their concerns so as not to be seen as the Leftist
hippy, the oversensitive queer or the angry black woman.
They are the trans teenagers who don't correct their
obnoxious uncles who insist on using the wrong gender
pronouns at the Christmas get-together. The overqualified
woman who lets her male colleagues mansplain how to
reboot the server. It's the black person in the office who
bites their tongue through the 'almost the same colour as
you now, Keisha!' shit their supervisor always pulls when
he gets back from a week in Lanzarote. Sometimes it's just
easier to keep your head down and get on with it.

But that is not the takeaway from this outrage autopsy.

Curbing your outrage is not about settling for less.
Nor is it about stifling social and political progress. It isn't
about silencing the outspoken, restraining the free-willed
or making your plight more palatable in the eyes of the
oppressors. It is not about being a subservient cog in a

system that has been rigged for you to fail, and it's certainly not asking you to unlearn the centuries of rebellion that have accorded us our twenty-first-century civil liberties.

As long as oppression continues to exist, outrage will too – and rightly so. This book is not a list of reasons to halt your protests. Of course not. That would be like society holding your head under water and me rolling my eyes at your submerged struggle. Quite the contrary. I urge you *not* to interpret this as an instruction to contain your intolerance.

We don't need to care less; we just need to care better. Because if we pursued severe social injustices as fervently as we did every insignificant faux pas that wafts under our noses, our communities would be far better places. But instead we assemble around life's dissatisfactions and wonder why the only thing we can negotiate is a half-decent phone upgrade.

As I looked back on my journey with this book, I worried that our outrage was achieving even less than I'd initially feared. I'd encountered dozens of instances of mass fury over the past two years, but none had even remotely moved society on. Sure, we'd used it to call out corporations like Target, cancel strangers like Rachel Dolezal, create villains like Katie Hopkins, and get a few broadcasters fired. But I was beginning to realise that we are fooling ourselves into thinking that we're progressive because our outrage appears to be so buoyant online. For all our many tweets of outrage, angry blog posts, Facebook rants, brand boycotts and performative protests, what progress has been made? What return has there been on the millions of hours we have collectively invested in digital outrage? How are you even meant to respond to an outraged Facebook post anyway? Do I 'like' it? Or does that I mean I like what has outraged you? Isn't a thumbs-up a bit sarky for your #MeToo confessional? For the love of God, somebody explain the rules!

'Don't boo. Vote,' said Barack Obama in 2016.

Those simple words, spontaneously uttered at the Democratic National Convention, tell us everything we need to change about outrage.

The problem is, we wave our fists at our issues instead of taking a swing at them. We intellectualise society's faults, dissecting them on our Facebook pages, debating them on Twitter and untangling them in blogs, feeding into our self-serving agendas of perception and popularity – but rarely do we make the necessary strides to affect change in the real world. We boo, but we don't vote. And if I learned anything writing this book it is that we need to transfer our resistance from the Internet to the real world and reignite the purposeful outrage that drove society forward in the offline era.

Even habitual provocateur Katie Hopkins conceded to me 'we'd both probably argue that me gobbing off on Twitter is not gonna change anything. So how do you impact or effect real change? That is the challenge for Hopkins.' And if the bigots who speak in the third person have figured it out, it's about time we did too.

So rather than using our narcissistic apps simply to narrate our experiences in this twenty-first-century social cesspit, it's time to figure out how we're actually going to get out of it. Let's stop talking about what we're going through and work out where we're going to! Perhaps by extending the reach of our tribes, we can ensure that our voices reverberate far beyond the confines of our own echo chambers. For with 3 billion of us actively using social media every day and 90.4 per cent of the world's millennials engaging with at least one digital platform, we certainly have the manpower to make a difference with our outrage. If four teenagers from Greensboro could spark a revolution at a lunch counter in Woolworth's, surely we can do just as much with the world's greatest innovation in the palm of our hands?

But if we are to use the progressive power of the Internet to truly rediscover the currency in our outrage, then there are a few things we need to change first...

First (and it's abundantly clear): We must reacquaint ourselves with the block button. Immediately. Katie Hopkins thinks we were bonkers to pay her so much attention. So sometimes it is necessary to switch off. If it's causing you undue stress: block. If a debate has reached an impasse: block. If you have to question whether or not to block: block.

Second: Refrain from embarking on moral expeditions just because you've convinced yourself that you're supposed to. It is time to stop pretending that you care about every fucking thing. Stop forcing yourself to be woke. We can all see that you're faking it.

Third: fact-check, fact-check and then fact-check again. Our judgement has been impaired by a social media phenomenon that has blurred the lines between what's real and fake, encouraging us to be fast instead of factual. Take your time. Read the article, not just the clickbait headline. Verify sources. Kick the tyres before you jump on the bandwagon. Or you'll find yourself campaigning against the removal of a fountain that was never actually going anywhere.

And fourth: when it comes to expressing outrage, we must have these conversations offline as well as on. We must be active as well as vocal. When dragging Ryanair for their mishandling of a racist passenger, we must send formal emails or letters as well as vengeful tweets.

When Stephanie Yeboah noticed a diversity problem on the women's fashion website PrettyLittleThing in 2018, she was invited to the company's Manchester headquarters to discuss their lack of plus-size representation. The following year, PrettyLittleThing unveiled a plus-size campaign modelled by dark-skinned black models. It was a change that had been prompted by a conversation as well as a call-out.

And a few months after our first chat, I received a jubilant email from Stop Funding Hate's Richard Wilson, who was keen to update me on a significant development. The organisation's focused outrage and composed campaigning had contributed to new measures being taken by the United Nations, who had released proposals for 'stopping allocation of public funding or material support to media outlets that systematically promote intolerance, xenophobia, racism and other forms of discrimination towards migrants'. In other words, the UN wasn't gonna stand for any more of the bullshit. 'This is the first time that the idea of ethical advertising as a mechanism for making media hate unprofitable has been recognised in an international agreement,' Richard told me. The outraged were launching a takedown of the outrage-mongers and it had taken over a year of engagement between Stop Funding Hate and the United Nations.

Still think your forty-eight hours of fury will have a lasting effect?

Sometimes we need to call people out on their fuckery. Grave misdeeds shouldn't, by any means, go unchecked. But if we are to avoid becoming one embarrassingly ineffectual voice of dissent, it is time to realise that outrage is not a novelty and start treating it like the weapon of progress it once was.

So the next time you think of frivolously investing your outrage, ask yourself: is this worth my time or my energy? Is it an outrage venture that will pay more than just performative dividends? Or am I simply spending recklessly? Do I actually have an axe to grind or do I just like the idea of standing for something?

Purposeful outrage can allow us to make headway in a world flooded with injustice. So I implore you to be outraged with dogged ambition, with fervour and tenacity. Create constructive tension. Pick your battles and then fight them tirelessly, with unrelenting resolve and clear-headed certainty. Find your motivation in truths rather than trends.

I will never relinquish the power of my outrage. I am simply learning to use it wisely, and I suggest you do too. Make outrage great again.

ACKNOWLEDGEMENTS

Writing a book will swallow any semblance of confidence you have, so I can say with absolute certainty that I am now a shadow of the person I once was.

I'd like to thank the people who helped to drag this book over the finish line when it was in its 'my knees are caving in, I'm not gonna make it' stage of the race.

My editor Alexis Kirschbaum, whose 'I think we're getting there' emails still sit tauntingly in my inbox giving me PTSD. You are truly a gem and I am very grateful for this opportunity. Thank you so much for believing in me and for giving me the freedom to figure this book out.

Thank you to Anna Vaux, the co-pilot who helped me land this book when I lost sight of the runway, I am forever indebted to you for your patience and guidance in the latter stages of this journey. You have motivated me in more ways than I can ever truly thank you for. ('This is a good start' will really put things into perspective when you think you've already finished).

Maya Wolfe-Robinson at the *Guardian* for giving my writing its first platform. Your belief in me is the only reason I was able to start writing this book. Thank you for lighting the flame.

My remarkable wife Lina, for not rolling her eyes when I abandoned our family holiday to write the outrage article. You had the patience of Job while I wrote this book (and rewrote it, then wrote it again) and I couldn't have got through it without your unwavering support, encouragement and noodle soup.

My son, Camden, who grew from a bouncing baby to a talkative toddler in the time it took me to write these chapters – you are the greatest motivation I could have ever asked for. Please don't grow up to be somebody who argues with strangers online.

To my dear friends for checking in on me when I disappeared into my laptop for months on end. Tania, Tasha, Francesca, Sabrina, Anneka, Robbie, Lucy, Cem – I'm available again for drinks, dinners, birthdays, weddings and any other plans I may have flaked on in the past two years. (I really meant it when I said: 'I'm writing a book.')

My incredibly supportive mum and dad – the greatest of role models. I couldn't ask for better parents. (Mum, those after-school spelling tests you insisted on giving us have finally paid off. Thank you.)

My three favourite people in the whole world, my siblings: Jordan, Milan and Leyton. I hate to keep overachieving but wow, a published author, I'm not sure where this leaves the rest of you in the 'golden child' rankings.

For the next generation of kids in my family, who motivate me to walk this earth with care: Sydney, Nova, Zion, Taelan, Zora, Isa and all my cousins. I love you all endlessly.

To the management at the BBC for supporting and encouraging my writing – Bob, James, Mark, Janine, thank you so much. And I must stress, 'these views are entirely mine and not those of my employers'.

To the many people that contributed to this book with interviews, emails, coffees, video calls, funny tweets, hate mail and the like – thank you for helping me colour inside the lines.

To the relentlessly and purposefully outraged – Black Lives Matter, Time's Up, Stonewall and everyone single movement striving to make things better for people like me – a million times thank you.

And to my secondary-school English teacher, Ms D'Silva, who told me I was a great writer – this one is for you.

In loving memory of my beloved grandma, who fell asleep while I wrote this book... Francoise Drysdale.

ABOUT THE AUTHOR

Ashley 'Dotty' Charles is the host of the BBC Radio 1Xtra *Breakfast Show* and the co-presenter of BBC One's *Sounds Like Friday Night*. She is the first solo female to host 1Xtra *Breakfast*. Under her rap alias Amplify Dot, she made British music history as the first female MC to sign a major-label album deal. She lives in London.

NOTE ON THE TYPE

The text of this book is set in Perpetua. This typeface is an adaptation of a style of letter that had been popularised for monumental work in stone by Eric Gill. Large scale drawings by Gill were given to Charles Malin, a Parisian punch-cutter, and his hand-cut punches were the basis for the font issued by Monotype. First used in a private translation called 'The Passion of Perpetua and Felicity', the italic was originally called Felicity.